knots

knots

A practical step-by-step guide to tying over 100 knots

GORDON PERRY

Grange
BOOKS

AN OCEANA BOOK

Published by Grange Books
an imprint of Grange Books Plc
The Grange
Kingsnorth Industrial Estate
Hoo, nr. Rochester
Kent ME3 9ND
www.grangebooks.co.uk

1-84013-493-3

This book is produced by
Oceana Books
6 Blundell Street
London N7 9BH

QUMTBOK

Designer: Peter Laws
Editor: Alex Revell
Photography: Celia Peterson, Gordon Perry
Illustration: Peter Owen, Heike Löwenstein, Heather McCarry

Manufactured in Singapore by
Pica Digital Pte. Ltd

Printed in Singapore by
Star Standard Industries Pte. Ltd

Publisher's Note
This book is intended for use as an introduction to knot tying.
Readers are strongly advised to seek advice from a qualified
professional before using particular knots for climbing, rescue
work or dangerous activities that could result in damage to
equipment or personal injury.

CONTENTS

B I N D I N G   K N O T S   7 0 - 9 7

H I T C H E S   9 8 - 1 4 1

L O O P S   1 4 2 - 1 8 5

M I S C E L L A N E O U S   &   D E C O R A T I V E   K N O T S   1 8 6 - 2 1 5

INTRODUCTION

The use of thread, string, cord, lines and ropes in our everyday lives and in outdoor pursuits is made easier and safer if we have some knowledge of cordage, and how to tie the appropriate knots in it. Cordage is made from natural or man-made fibres and is laid up in strands or braids. All cordage is weakened to some extent by tying knots in it.

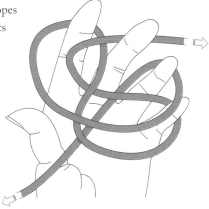

Knots are divided into the following groups: Bends (to join); Hitches (to attach); Stopper Knots (to stop unravelling or unreeving); Binding Knots (to bind) and Loop Knots (to form fixed or running loops). Having learned how to form each knot, take time to learn more about it. Test the knot in materials of different types and thickness; pull each knot about to discover how secure it is, and whether or not it could inadvertently come undone. Show your knots to other people – it is amazing how much you learn by teaching.

Knot books, like first aid books, abound, but each one offers something different – new discoveries, alternative methods, and so on. Like first aid, a basic knowledge of knots and ropework can also save lives.

In this book, the author outlines a selected range of knots that are useful in practical situations, together with some decorative and less well-known knots which are intended to inspire the imagination and

help while away those times when you shelter from the storm…

In addition, the construction of rope and materials used in cordage are explained, and there are many useful knotting tips. All the knots in this book can be tied without the use of special tools, which is why splicing has been limited to three-strand ropes (leaving the braids and plaits to more specialist publications).

Because the names of knots have acquired many different variations across the geographical, cultural and occupational spheres in which they are used, some alternative names have been included to help with identification. In

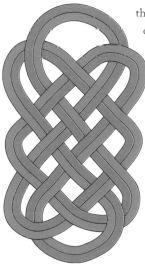

the home or garden, aboard your yacht, boat or canoe, at camp, on the water's edge, in remote countryside, on the farm or in the stable, this book will be an invaluable companion to those who wish to learn or refresh their knot tying skills.

Some knots in this book can be used to safeguard life – particularly those used for climbing and descent purposes. Learn how to tie these knots using this book, but do not put them into practice without supervision or proper training by a qualified instructor.

THE STRUCTURE OF ROPE

Stranded rope

Stranded rope is formed using natural fibres or man-made filaments of materials that have been twisted together to form yarns. Yarns are twisted together to form strands, and strands twisted together to make rope.

If you look at a piece of three-strand laid rope, you will find that it is either right-hand or Z-laid (no matter which way up you hold it, the strands appear to twist upwards and to the right) or left-hand or S-laid (the strands twist upwards and to the left). In the more common Z-laid rope, the first group of fibres are twisted to the right to form a right-hand yarn. Two or more yarns – depending on the size of rope required – are twisted together as left-hand laid strands, and the strands are then twisted together to the right to form right-hand or Z-laid rope.

Z-laid rope spirals up and to the right (above)

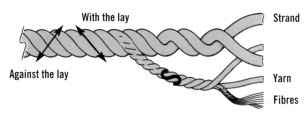

With the lay

Against the lay

Strand

Yarn

Fibres

S-laid strand spirals up and to the left (left)

Multi-plait rope (above)

Multi-plait rope

This consists of four (or six) pairs of strands. Two (or three) pairs are Z-laid and the other two (or three) pairs are S-laid. The strands are then plaited to form a rope.

Braided rope

Braided rope is formed in several different ways with fibres or filaments of materials. At the centre of the rope is a core, which can be single, twisted or plaited. Over the core is a cover, usually formed with an eight- or 16-plait weave. A further covering or sheath, normally for ease of handling, is sometimes added also using an eight- or 16-plait weave.

When a woven core stands alone it is generally referred to as "hollow braid". A woven core and cover is known as "braid on braid" or "double braid". Specific descriptions, such as "16-plait with three-strand core", or makers' trade names, such as "Marlowbraid" are also used. The number of combinations is too great to list here but, if you need to know more, the Internet and rope manufacturer's catalogues are both good sources of information. Due to the ever-increasing demands for excellence, it is becoming popular for manufacturers to combine more than one material in the construction of ropes, especially in braided ropes used for climbing and competitive sailing.

Braided rope (above)

CHOOSING ROPES

Your choice of cordage will, in an ideal situation, be made from experience, technical advice, regulations, and cost. However, it is sometimes necessary to use whatever is available, in which case *safety* should be your first consideration.

When buying rope, especially where the safety of life might depend on it, always seek professional advice, and "buy the best you can't afford". Obtain and keep a record of the manufacturer's data on each rope, including: manufacturer's name; date of production; material (sometimes found on a tape embedded as a fibre in one of the strands); strength or average breaking load; safe working load (approximately 10 per cent of the strength); weight and stretch. In addition, manufacturers have available, on request, a whole host of other technical and chemical data. The important thing to remember is that all this information applies only to *new* ropes. Always make allowances for rope that has been used, and check carefully for signs of damage or rot.

In situations where a rope may be subjected to shock loading, such as moorings, tow ropes and safety lines, choose a dynamic material like nylon or polyester. For static lines, such as halyards, guys, stays or lines that must not stretch, use low-stretch High Modulus Polyethylene (HMPE), or pre-stretched rope.

A wide range of modern cordage manufactured by Marlow ropes (right)

MATERIALS USED IN CORDAGE

Natural fibres

These are not very prominent today, but most are still available, especially sisal and cotton. Natural-fibre ropes are made using the bast fibres of plants such as cotton (cotton), cannabis sativa (hemp), jute plant (jute), coconut (coir) or leaf fibres from plants such as cactus-like agave (sisal) and abaca or wild banana plant (manila).

Man-made fibres

The most prolific man-made materials used in rope production today are polyamides, polyester, polypropylene and polyethylene.

Polyamides (PA), more commonly known as nylon or perlon, consist of a very fine white fibre. Nylon is the strongest rope material when dry, but loses some strength when wet. It has good elasticity and does not float, making it ideal for use in berthing hawsers, tow ropes and anchor warps and lines which are liable to shock loading.

Polyester (PES, PET) materials, including

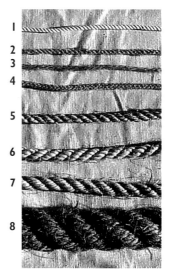

Natural fibre ropes

1 Cotton	5 Manila
2 Hemp	6 Sisal S-laid
3 Jute soft laid	7 Sisal Z-laid
4 Jute braided	8 Coir or Bass

dacron, terylene and vectran, also consist of fine white fibres. Commonly made into both stranded and braided rope, polyester is almost as strong as nylon and retains its strength, wet or dry. It is supple and hard wearing, with about half the stretch found in nylon – even less if Liquid Crystal Polymer (LCP) or "pre-stretched" by the

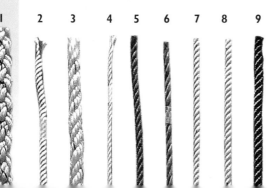

Stranded fibre cordage
1 Nylon eight-strand multi-plait
2 Cotton
3 Spun-staple polypropylene
4 Polypropylene cord
5 Monofilament polypropylene
6 Split-film polypropylene
7 Polyester
8 Nylon
9 Polyester

manufacturer. Polyester is often used together with polypropylene to form mixed-fibre ropes, and in rope covers where its resistance to abrasion is necessary to protect more delicate core materials.

Polypropylene (PP) is used primarily to make replica natural fibre and inexpensive general-purpose rope. It is constructed using single (or mono) filaments, which produce a smooth wax-like finish to stranded ropes. Polypropylene can also be fibrillated and dyed to resemble natural fibres, and then made into rope that looks like hemp or tarred rope. Spun-staple fibres are sometimes used, which result in a hairy finish to the rope to produce a good grip. Split-film construction is often used in the most inexpensive lines. All polypropylene ropes float and most are brightly coloured, making them ideal for use as lifelines.

Polyethylene (PE) rope is made from white or coloured coarse fibres. It floats, is supple and is popular in the sea fishing industry. Advances in polyethylene technology have also produced an extremely strong family of fine fibres known collectively as High Modulus Polyethylene (HMPE). Ropes in this group can be as strong as steel wire ropes of equal size. Their light weight, low stretch properties and total resistance to water make them ideal for use in sailing dinghies and high performance yachts.

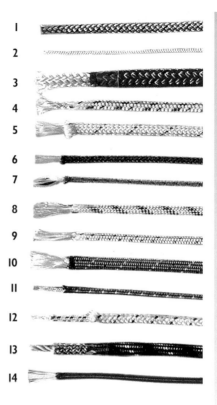

1
2
3
4
5
6
7
8
9
10
11
12
13
14

Braided man-made fibre cordage
1 Polypropylene hollow braid
2 Nylon hollow braid
3 Nylon braided core, polyester cover
4 Polyester braid-on-braid
5 Polyester low-twist core, polyester matt cover
6 Polyester multifilament, polyester matt cover
7 Polyester low-twist core, polyester cover
8 Polyester three-strand core, polyester cover
9 Dyneema core, polyester cover
10 Spectra/dyneema core, open weave cover, smooth woven sheath
11 Dyneema braid core, polyester cover
12 Dyneema braid core, woven cover, sheath of matt polyester
13 Monofilament polypropylene, acrylic cover, matt polyester sheath
14 Rubber multi-strand, polyester cover

CARE & MAINTENANCE

Apart from the fact that rope is quite expensive, your life – or that of others – could be at risk if cordage is not cared for properly. Similarly, your equipment – be it an expensive yacht or the fly on the end of a fishing line – could be damaged or lost. The following lists of DOs and DON'Ts will help maintain the condition of your rope.

DO:
- Check for damage before use;
- Keep all types of cordage clean;
- Wash rope with non-detergent soap;
- Rinse rope exposed to salt water with fresh water as often as possible and always before stowing;
- Coil rope properly to avoid kinking;
- Remove any knots that are not in use;
- Lubricate (saliva is best) monofilament lines before pulling up knots – this prevents burn damage;
- Store all types of cordage loosely coiled and hung off the ground.

DON'T:
- Subject ropes to excessive friction – burning damages all types of fibres;
- Drag ropes through sand, grit, oil or over rough surfaces;
- Apply a load to a rope that is kinked;
- Stand on ropes – as well as transferring dirt and grit from the bottom of footwear, it can damage the fibres;
- Overload or overstretch a rope or bungee cord – apart from being dangerous, it will distort and eventually break, or be permanently weakened;
- Leave exposed to the sun unnecessarily.

Cable-laid ropes arranged for display as a museum piece

TOOLS USED IN ROPEWORK

A knife is the most basic tool for cutting cordage; other methods of cutting include scissors, small shears and a heated blade, or wire (for synthetics). A pair of pliers will be useful for operations where the fingers are not strong enough or might be cut. Forceps can be used for delicate and fancy work where the fingers are too big or clumsy.

Specific to ropework, fids are used to open out the strands of ropes for splicing. They are usually made from very close grained wood – such as lignum vitae – or from steel with a small wooden hand protector – such as the Swedish fid. Wire loop tools are generally hand made by knot tyers, and used mainly for drawing the working ends of cords through fancy ropework.

Whipping twine is used to form whippings, stops and seizing; it can also be used for sewing. Adhesive tape also makes an excellent temporary whipping, especially when cutting ropes, and can be used for identification purposes. A butane gas lighter, cigarette lighter or matches can be used to seal the ends of synthetic fibre cordage.

Specialist tools include: the marline-spike for splicing wire; hollow fids and loop tools for splicing braided ropes; and the Sailmaker's palm and needle.

Tools used in knotting and ropework

A Swedish fid	H Wire loop
B Marlinespike	I Adhesive tape
C Pliers	J Whipping twine
D Marlinespike	K Sailmaker's twine
E Small Swedish fid	L Butane gas lighter
F Marlinespike	M Forceps
G Wooden fid	N Rigging knife

SELECTING KNOTS

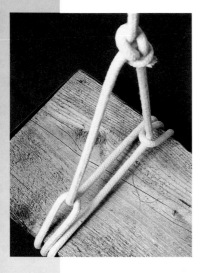

At the beginning of each section in this book are listed common uses for the knots in that section. However, selecting the best knot for the job depends on a number of additional factors.

Security

• Will the knot hold in the material used?

• Do the working ends need additional tucks, or should they be left long or secured?

• Is the size of the material a factor (some knots will not hold in very large or stiff rope)?

The Oklahoma Hitch – a secure and stable knot for supporting a wooden plank (left)

Stability

• Will the knot collapse, "spill" or "capsize" when under stress, if it is subjected to snagging against another object or when not under load?

Strength

• How much will the knot weaken the cordage in which it is tied?

Lines weakened by knots will, more often than not, break at the point where the standing part enters the knot. Commonly used knots can weaken a rope from 30–60 per cent of its unknotted strength, while splicing retains most, if not all, of the strength of a rope.

An Eye Splice will retain most, if not all, of the strength of the rope in which it is tied (right)

TERMS USED IN ROPEWORK

Some of the more common terms used in knotting and ropework are shown here – eye, loop, turn, bight, standing part, working end, whipping and seizing. Other terms include: with the lay (p.10); against the lay (p.10); hard laid (p.217); soft laid (p.219); right-hand or Z-laid rope (p.219) and left-hand or S-laid rope (p.219). The term cordage is used to encompass any suitable thread, string, cord, line or rope.

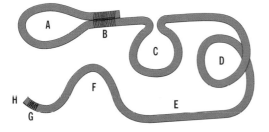

Rope terms
A Eye
B Seizing
C Loop
D Turn
E Standing part
F Bight
G Whipping
H Working end

HOW TO USE THIS BOOK

The sequence diagrams that accompany the descriptions of knots are intended to be self-explanatory. The arrows indicate the direction in which the working ends or bights should be pulled, threaded or held, while the dotted lines indicate intermediate positions or the path a working end will take to arrive at the next step.

Always follow the order indicated and check that the under/over sequence of a knot is correct before pulling it up. Each knot in the book is accompanied by an icon to provide, at a glance, the different purposes for which that knot can be used. These include general purpose, camping, climbing and caving, boating and sailing, fishing and horsemanship.

 General purpose

 Camping

 Climbing and caving

 Boating and sailing

 Fishing

 Horsemanship

STOPPER KNOTS

Stopper knots are used either in the end of a rope to stop it from unlaying or fraying, or as a handhold or decoration. They can also be made in a rope that has been unlaid, the knot tied and then laid up again, normally as a handhold or foothold, but often just for decoration.

Uses for stopper knots include:

To stop the end of a sewing thread passing through the weave –
Overhand Knot (p.20)
Slipped Overhand Knot (p.21)

To decorate the end of a robe cord or light pull –
Multiple Overhand Knot (p.22)
Heaving Line Knot (p.28)

Make a handhold or foothold at the end of a rope –
Oysterman's Knot (p.24)
Stevedore's Knot (p.25)

To stop the end of a halyard passing through a block –
Figure-of-Eight Knot (p.26)

To weight the end of a line for throwing –
Heaving Line Knot (p.28)
Monkey's Fist (p.30)

To make a round key fob –
Monkey's Fist (p.30)

To start an upward weave or plait –
Wall Knot (p.32)

To start a back splice or downward weave or plait –
Crown Knot (p.33)

To make a decorative spiral knot with two or more cords –
Matthew Walker Knot (p.34)

To make a handhold or foothold in the standing part of a Stranded rope –
Matthew Walker Knot (p.34)
Diamond Knot (p.36)

To decorate the end of a stair or barrier rope –
Manrope Knot (p.38)

OVERHAND KNOT

Also known as: *Simple Knot; Thumb Knot*

The Overhand Knot is the simplest of the stopper knots

This knot turns up everywhere (particularly in tangles) and is shown here in its simplest form, tied in the end of a line as a stopper knot. It can be used in the end of single or double small diameter cord, line or even sewing thread, either as a small stopper knot or to prevent the ends from unravelling. Tighten the knot by pulling on the standing part while cupping the bight in the other hand.

Also related to this knot is the Half Knot, which forms the first part of the Reef Knot (p.72) that we tie in our shoelaces. The Reef Knot is tied using two ends and, as such, is classified as a binding knot.

Learn to tie this knot both right and left handed

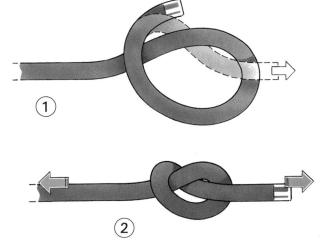

① ②

SLIPPED OVERHAND KNOT

If a large stopper knot is needed, the Slipped Overhand Knot can be used. This knot is often used in the end of cotton thread when hand sewing. The advantage of this knot over the Overhand Knot (p.20) is that it can be easily undone by pulling the working end.

The Slipped Overhand is another foundation knot the reader is advised to practice, as it will help in tying many of the other knots in this book. Take care not to confuse this knot with the Overhand Noose, where the Overhand Knot is tied in the working end around the standing part.

The Slipped Overhand Knot – a foundation for many other knots

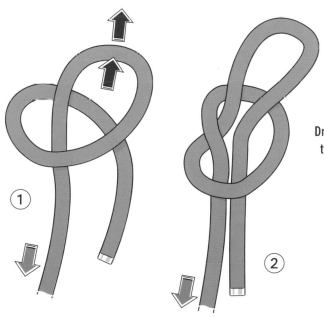

SLIPPED OVERHAND KNOT

Draw sewing twines over a block of beeswax before use on heavy materials

TOP TIP

MULTIPLE OVERHAND KNOT
Also known as: *Double Overhand Knot; Blood Knot*

A Multiple Overhand Knot as a decorative end to a cord

One stage up from the Overhand Knot (p.20) is the Double Overhand Knot, which, when pulled up by the same method as Overhand Knot will form a stopper knot with two turns around the standing part. By adding more turns, it now becomes a Multiple Overhand Knot, shown here with three tucks, but more are possible. The effect of using more than two tucks results in a more decorative knot, but does not enhance its ability as a stopper knot.

Make the loop large enough to allow the twists to lay straight before you commence pulling on the ends while gently twisting the standing part and the working end. Watch carefully how the knots form, because in material that does not slip easily it will be necessary to manoeuvre each turn carefully into position as the knot is pulled up. This is a handsome knot, which looks nice in the end of the waist cord of a robe or gown.

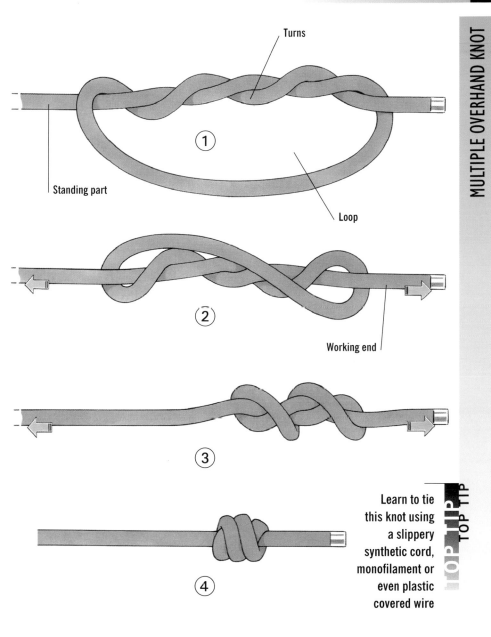

Turns

Standing part

Loop

(1)

(2)

Working end

(3)

(4)

Learn to tie
this knot using
a slippery
synthetic cord,
monofilament or
even plastic
covered wire

TOP TIP

OYSTERMAN'S KNOT

Clifford Ashley gave the the Oysterman's Knot its name in his book – *The Ashley Book of Knots* – after discovering it, apparently with no name, on board an oyster boat. It is simply tied by forming an Overhand Noose, passing the working end through the bight and pulling up using the standing part. When formed it has a wide flat base and is probably the best end stopper knot to use on tent guy-line runners and such like.

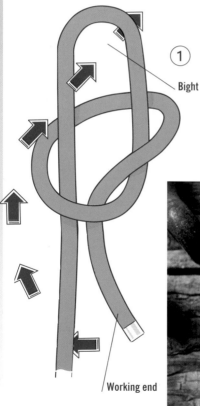

① Bight

② Standing part

Working end

The Oysterman's Knot, ideal for tent guy-line runners (right)

STEVEDORE'S KNOT
Also known as: *Figure Nine Knot*

The Stevedore's Knot forms a good temporary stopper knot, which is just as easy to tie (and untie) but a little bulkier than the Oysterman's Knot (p.24). To pull up, cup the knot in one hand and pull the standing part. This knot makes a good end stopper for a conker (horse chestnut) string or for stringing beads. It is easier to form if the working end is passed around the standing part (rather than twisting the bight) before it is passed through the bight.

The Stevedore's Knot – ideal for use in thin line

(1)

Standing part

Working end

(2)

FIGURE-OF-EIGHT KNOT

Also known as: *Flemish Knot*

If I could teach only one knot to a person, this would be it. In its simplest form, the Figure-of-Eight Knot is perhaps the most commonly used of all the stopper knots. It can also be configured to provide a multitude of bends, hitches and loops that are practical and safe. As a stopper knot, it is more bulky than the Overhand Knot (p.20) and easier to untie, which is probably why it is used extensively in sailing to stop rope ends running through blocks. Tighten the knot by pulling the standing part only, holding the bights in a cupped hand so that the knot pulls up as shown (right). If both the standing part and working end are pulled, a decorative knot forms. With excessive shaking, especially in a sheet that has been let fly, this may even come undone.

TOP TIP

This knot is ideal for use under a swing seat. Middle the rope and tie two Figure-of-Eight Knots (pulled up as stopper knots) to form a square support arrangement

The Figure-of-Eight Knot, used to stop the end of the rope from passing through the block

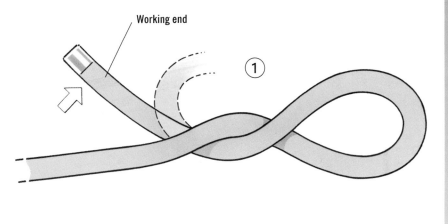

Working end

①

②

Working end

Standing part

Figure-of-Eight formation

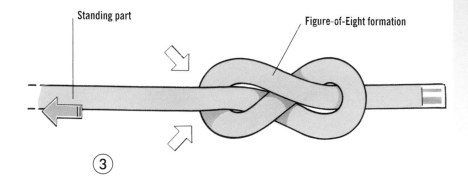

③

HEAVING LINE KNOT
Also known as: *Franciscan Knot; Monk's Knot*

A quick, easy and safe method of weighting the end of a line for throwing. Normally used in the end of a heaving line, as the name suggests. The knotted end of the line can be thrown from a boat to the dockside or over a wall, around the branch of a tree, and so on, and the other end bent on to a heavier mooring or climbing rope. Used in the end of decorative cord it forms a neat arrangement of circles around the standing part so that the cord hangs well. Hold the turns and pull on the standing part to tighten the knot.

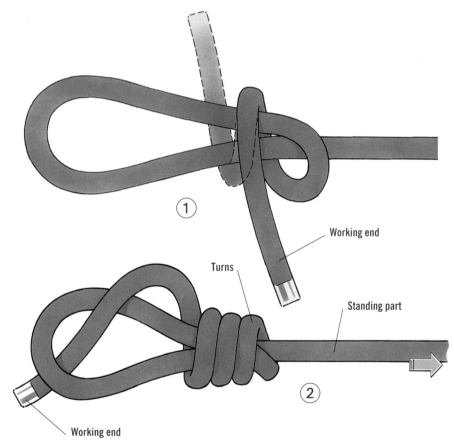

Working end

Turns

Standing part

Working end

A greater number of turns will increase the weight of the Heaving Line Knot

③

Always secure the standing
end of a heaving line to a
berthing line or hawser,
guard rail or other static
object before throwing
the weighted end

TOP TIP

MONKEY'S FIST

The Monkey's Fist weighting the end of a heaving line

The Monkey's Fist was designed to form a weight on the end of a heaving line. However, the symmetrical pattern formed by this knot has also made it popular as a decorative knot for key-ring fobs, light pull cords and similar functional items. When tying the knot, leave plenty of room to make each of the final tucks. The working end can be either spliced or whipped to the standing part, or tucked inside the knot.

TOP TIP

A large pebble covered with a Monkey's Fist makes an attractive door stop

To tuck inside, form a stopper knot in the end and tighten the Monkey's Fist over it by working back towards the standing part. Pull up a little of the slack at a time, otherwise the knot is likely to loose its shape. If the knot is being used as a heaving line weight, *never* put anything heavy or hard inside the knot. For decoration, any spherical object can be used in the centre of the knot – marbles, golf balls, wooden beads, etc. – but you may need to use more turns to cover the object completely. The end of the cord or rope can be tucked inside the knot out of sight.

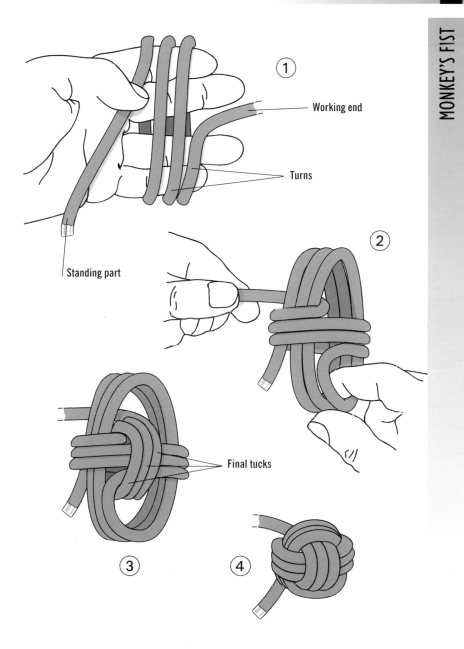

(1)

Working end

Turns

Standing part

(2)

Final tucks

(3)   (4)

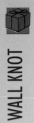
WALL KNOT

"Forming a Wall makes the ends stand tall." The Wall Knot is rarely used on its own, but is worth learning as it forms the basis of many other knot formations. The Wall Knot, with a Crown Knot (p.33) tied on top makes an attractive alternative to the Turk's Head, and can be doubled or trebled to increase its bulk. Continuous "walling" can also be used to cover cylindrical objects.

A Wall Knot formed with four strands

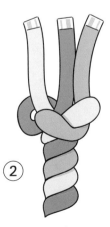

TOP TIP

Use a Constrictor Knot (p.76) to form a temporary whipping around three-strand rope

CROWN KNOT

"When forming the Crown, the strands go down." Like the Wall Knot (p.32), the Crown Knot is rarely used alone. It is perhaps most frequently used to form the foundation of a Back Splice (p.194), or to form Sennits (p.208–211). The formation of a three-stranded Wall Knot is depicted (right), but more strands can be used (below).

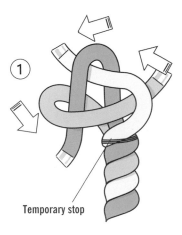

Temporary stop

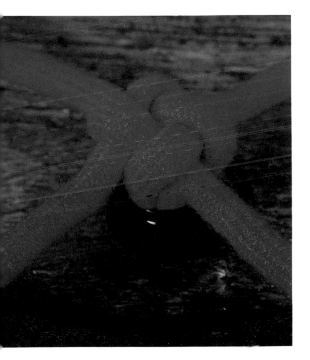

The Crown Knot can be tied with three or more strands

TOP TIP

Use temporary whippings or adhesive tape to hold the strands and to stop the strand ends from unlaying; it also makes them easier to pass under the strands of a rope while splicing

CROWN KNOT

MATTHEW WALKER KNOT

The Matthew Walker Knot forms a decorative stopper knot in, or near the end of, a rope

TOP TIP

Learn this knot with three strands, then increase to five, six or more as your skill improves

The Matthew Walker knot is a handsome stopper knot which can be inserted in any stranded rope that will re-lay back to its original form; unfortunately many synthetic ropes will not re-lay. For decorative ropework, it can be formed in almost any number of strands of cord – which have been bound together – to make an attractive spiral knot. When pulling up, try to visualise the final form of the knot, be patient and work each strand carefully.

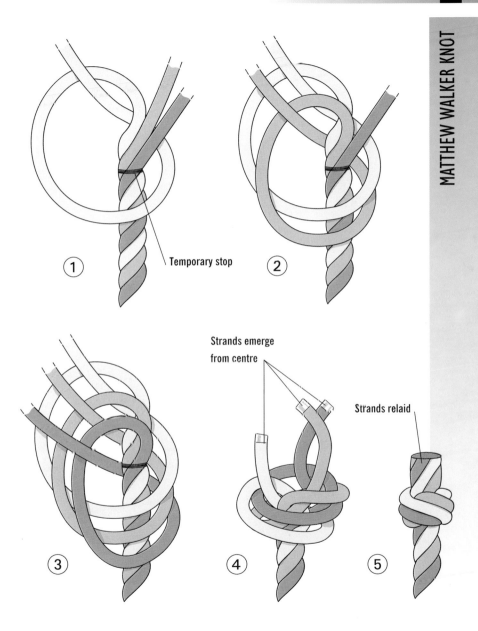

1 Temporary stop

2

Strands emerge
from centre

Strands relaid

3

4

5

DIAMOND KNOT

The Diamond Knot – an example of the Wall and Crown Knots being used together

The Diamond Knot is an attractive stopper knot for use in the standing part of a rope, rather than at the end. The rope should be stopped and the strands unlaid and whipped before the knot is tied. The strands emerging from the centre of the knot are then laid up again. The Diamond Knot is an example of the Crown Knot (p.33) and the Wall Knot (p.32) being used together.

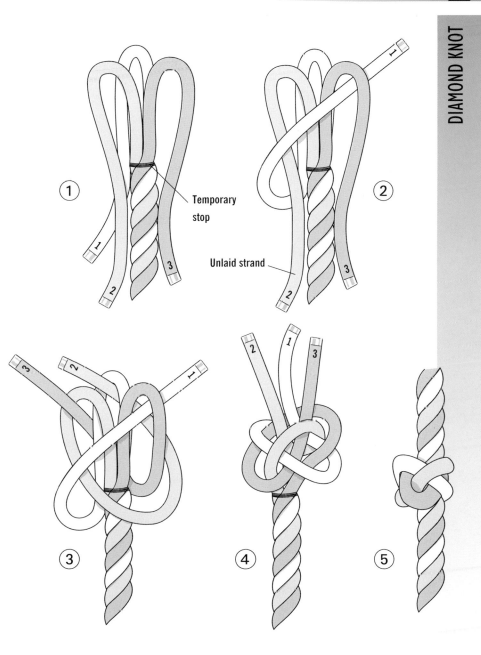

Temporary
stop

Unlaid strand

MANROPE KNOT

Also known as: *Tack Knot*

The Manrope Knot – as a decorative end to a barrier rope – enhancing the "Arts of a Sailor"

TOP TIP

To enhance the decorative appearance, cover each strand with canvas or coloured material and place a leather washer behind the knot as shown in the accompanying photograph

"First a Wall, then a Crown, double the lead and tuck the ends down". This handsome finish to the end of three- or four-strand rope is both practical and decorative. It can be used at the end of a swinging rope as a foot- or hand-hold, or to stop a lanyard slipping through the hand. For many years this knot has been a popular decorative stopper at the end of a rope used as a handrail or barrier (above).

Before unlaying the strands, measure at least 20 times the diameter of the rope from the end and add a temporary stop – a Constrictor Knot (p.76) or Whipping (p.90) – then tape or whip the ends of each strand. Begin with a Wall Knot (p.32) and follow with a Crown Knot (p.33). When the knot has been pulled up firmly, the ends can be spliced into the standing part using a tapered splice, which in turn can be covered with a Whipping. Alternatively, the ends can be cut off short up under the knot.

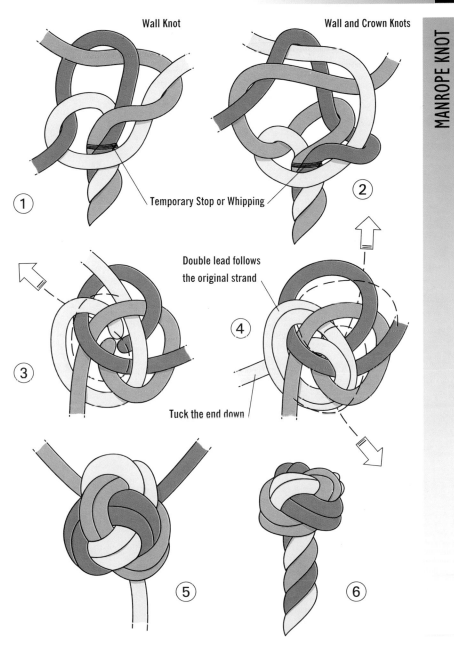

Wall Knot

Wall and Crown Knots

Temporary Stop or Whipping

① ②

Double lead follows
the original strand

④

③

Tuck the end down

⑤ ⑥

BENDS

To "bend" is a term used when joining two pieces of cordage together, normally as a temporary arrangement.

Uses for bends include:

To join two sections of tippet or leader –
Double Grinner Knot (p.42)

To join two lines of different thickness –
Sheet Bend (p.44)

To bend a messenger to rope that will be hauled over an obstruction –
Sheet Bend – One Way (p.46)

To join two lines together –
Fisherman's Knot (p.47)
Figure-of-Eight Bend (p.50)

To join two lines of monofilament or slippery material –
Double Fisherman's Knot (p.48)

To join two large or heavy lines –
Carrick Bend (p.52)

To join diverse material lines and bungee cord –
Ashley's Bend (p.54)
Hunter's Bend (p.56)

To join small lines and lacing –
Harness Bend (p.58)

To join monofilament and thin nylon line –
Blood Knot (p.60)

To join different size nylon and mono lines –
Water Knot (p.62)

To join fly line to braided backer –
Nail Knot (p.64)

To join a fly line to the butt end of a leader –
Needle Knot (p.66)

To join a heaving line/messenger to a large hawser –
Racking Bend (p.68)

To join two large ropes of the same or different size –
Bowline Bend (p.69)

DOUBLE GRINNER KNOT
Also known as: *Paragum Knot*

This knot is actually two Grinner Knots tied back to back as an effective way of joining together two sections of tippet or a leader. Lay the two lines parallel and tie the first Grinner (you may find it useful to peg or clip the second standing part and the working end together while doing this). Tighten the knot with a pair of forceps or pliers before tying the second Grinner. To complete, pull both standing parts to draw the knots together and cut back the working ends for neatness.

Two monofilament lines securely joined with the Double Grinner Knot

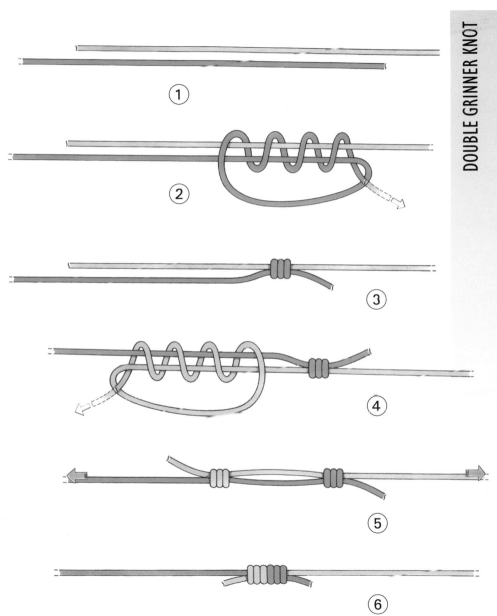

SHEET BEND
Also known as: *Common Bend*

Although this knot has its origins deep in the history of sail, when it was used to attach the sheets to the clew on a sail, the Sheet Bend has, for centuries, had all manner of other uses. It can be used to join two lines of different thickness provided the difference is not too great, in which case a Racking Bend (p.68) is more appropriate. The Sheet Bend can also be used to secure a rope to anything with an aperture, through which the line can be passed and the working end trapped under the standing part – for instance, with a hammock ring. In the absence of Ingafield clips, it can be used on the lower end of the tack line of a flag to bend it to the halyard. Another common use is in the knitting or repair of netting.

The Sheet Bend, used to join two lines of different thicknesses

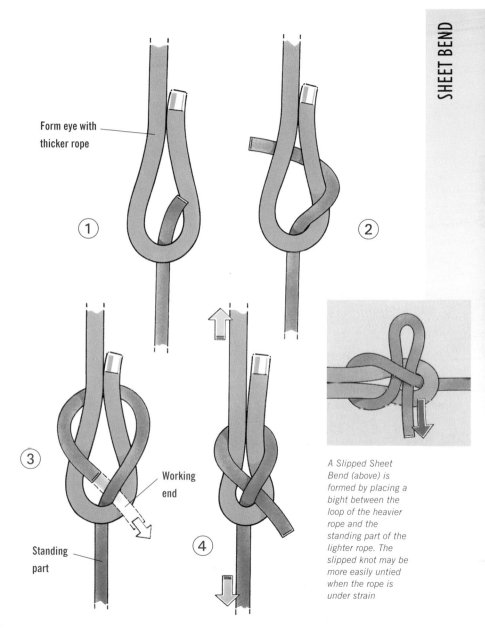

Form eye with
thicker rope

① ②

③

Working
end

Standing
part

④

A Slipped Sheet
Bend (above) is
formed by placing a
bight between the
loop of the heavier
rope and the
standing part of the
lighter rope. The
slipped knot may be
more easily untied
when the rope is
under strain

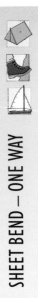

SHEET BEND – ONE WAY

The Sheet Bend – One Way can be pulled over an edge or obstruction without snagging

The Sheet Bend – One Way is used when joined ropes need to be hauled over edges or obstructions. Start by tying a Sheet Bend (p.44), then take the working end of the hauling line in front of its standing part and up through its own bight. By this method, both working ends are laid down alongside the rope being hauled, and are therefore less likely to snag on an obstruction.

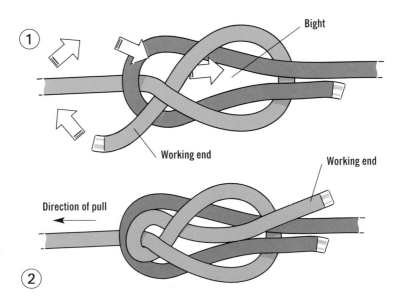

① **Bight**

Working end

② **Direction of pull** **Working end**

FISHERMAN'S KNOT

Also known as: *Angler's Knot; English Knot; Halibut Knot; Waterman's Knot*

The Fisherman's Knot – a reliable way to join two lines

The Fisherman's Knot – not to be confused with the Fisherman's Bend, (p.112) – is formed with two identical Overhand Knots (p.20), which are drawn together so that the short working ends of each lie in opposite directions. This is a safe and reliable way of joining two lines or small ropes of equal, or near equal, diameter. However, like all knots, it will weaken the lines in which it is tied.

FISHERMAN'S KNOT

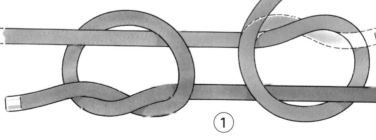

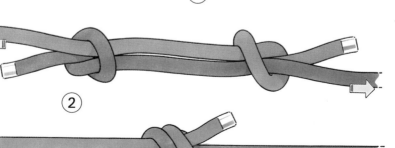

DOUBLE FISHERMAN'S KNOT

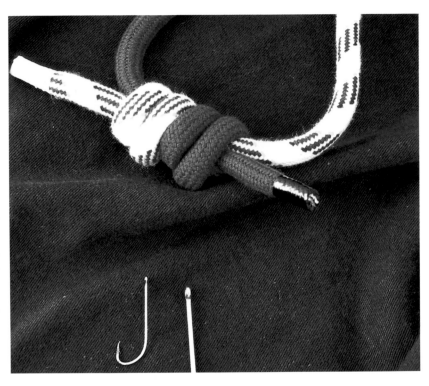

The Double Fisherman's Knot is secure, even in monofilament lines

TOP TIP

Tape or seize the working ends to the standing part for a neat finish, or to prevent them snagging on obstructions

No more complicated than the Fisherman's Knot (p.47), except that the overhand knots are doubled (p.22) to form a slightly more stable knot, especially in monofilament line. The overhand knots can also be trebled or quadrupled for added security.

DOUBLE FISHERMAN'S KNOT

1
Standing part
Working end

2
Rotate work
First Double Overhand Knot
Working end

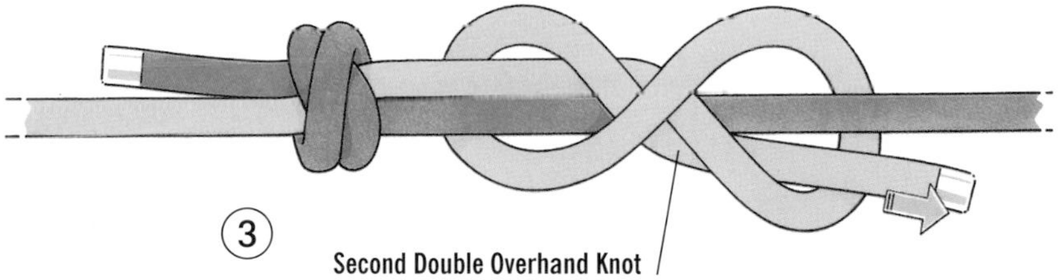

3
Second Double Overhand Knot

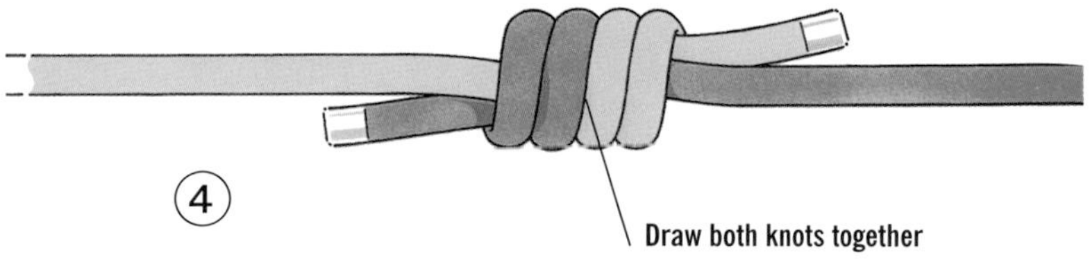

4
Draw both knots together

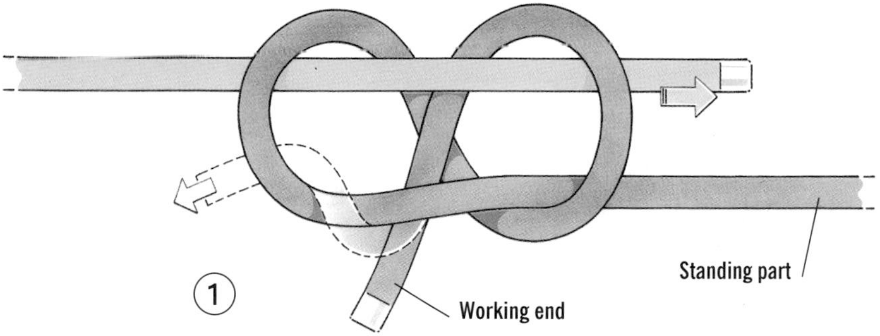

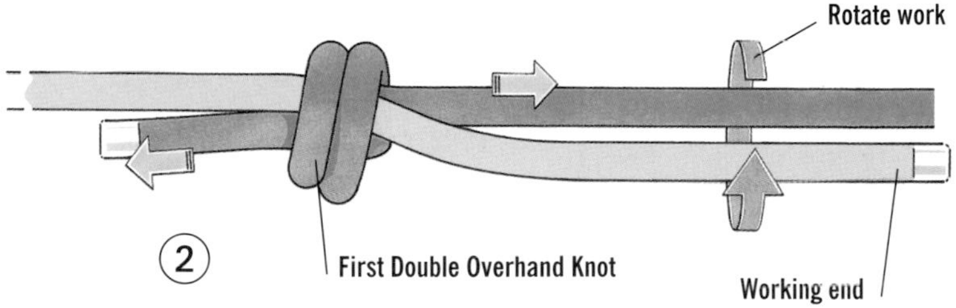

FIGURE-OF-EIGHT BEND

Also known as: *Flemish Bend*

The Figure-of-Eight Bend is one of the strongest and most stable bends currently used in cord and rope. It is easy to tie and, even after it has been under considerable strain, can be untied with a little persuasion.

Form a loosely tied Figure-of-Eight Knot (p.26) in Line A (step one). Insert the working end of Line B into the knot parallel to the working end of Line A (step two). Follow the lead around the knot so that the working end of Line B emerges alongside the standing part of Line A (step three). The working ends can be taped to the standing parts if necessary.

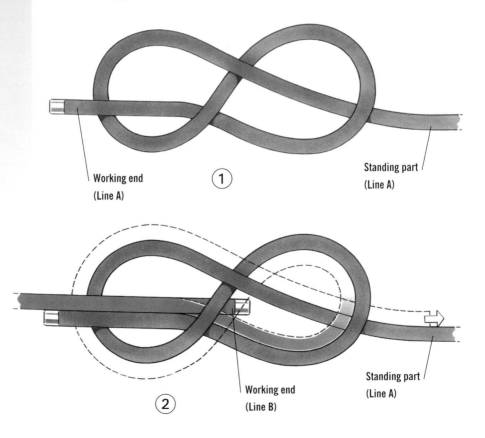

Working end
(Line A)

(1)

Standing part
(Line A)

Working end
(Line B)

(2)

Standing part
(Line A)

The Figure-of-Eight Bend, which can be untied even after it has been under considerable strain

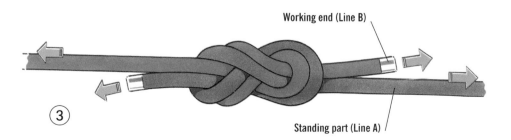

Working end (Line B)

③

Standing part (Line A)

CARRICK BEND

Join large-diameter ropes using a Carrick Bend

The Carrick Bend is mainly used for joining large-diameter ropes or hawsers, but is included in this book for completeness. It can be used to join two ropes of slightly dissimilar diameter, and should be pulled up using the standing parts. Where necessary, for instance to pass through bull rings, fairleads or around a capstan, the working ends should be seized to the standing parts. Note that the working ends emerge from the knot on different sides.

Tied with the working ends emerging from the same side of the knot, which allows it to be pulled up flat, the Carrick Bend becomes a decorative knot often found in macramé projects or on uniform braiding. In this form it is known as the Josephine Knot or Check Knot.

(1) Working end

Standing part

(2) Standing part

(3)

An attractive knot, known as the Japanese Parcel Knot (right), is tied in the same way as the Carrick Bend using double ends

ASHLEY'S BEND

Ashley's Bend forming the centre of a four-way bungee cord tie-down

It is only recently that this knot has been known as Ashley's Bend; in his book, *The Ashley Book of Knots*, Clifford Ashley writes it up as being original but doesn't give it a name. This knot has many uses – it can be used to join cordage, raffia, seagrass, and even such diverse materials as monofilament and bungee (shock) cord. It will accept pulling in any direction on any of the four ends. One particularly appropriate application using this feature is to form the centre of a four-way tie-down (above). One of the very few bends that is 100 per cent stable, it not only holds well but is easy to untie after being put under strain. To tie, form an Overhand Knot (p.20) with one rope, then pass the second rope through it (steps one and two). Pull gently on all four leads, then pull up the two standing parts to tighten the knot.

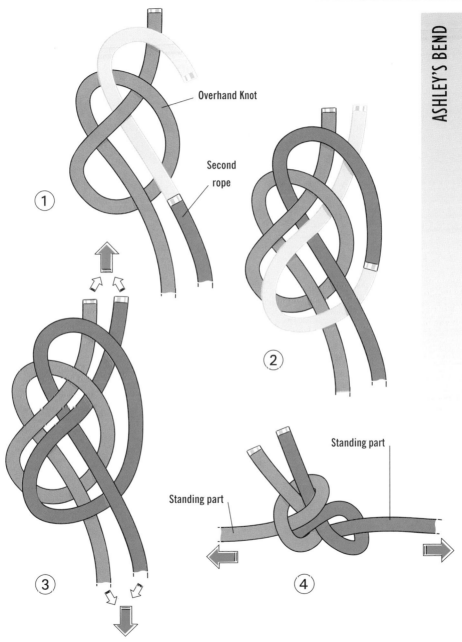

Overhand Knot

Second
rope

①

②

③

④

Standing part

Standing part

HUNTER'S BEND
Also known as: *Rigger's Bend*

The Hunter's Bend, named after Dr E Hunter

The Hunter's Bend was named after *The Times* published an article in 1978 claiming that Dr E Hunter had discovered a new knot. Subsequent correspondence established that the knot had already been published in 1950 as the Rigger's Bend – a discovery that lead to the formation of the International Guild of Knot Tyers (IGKT).

The Hunter's Bend is a stable knot with a good grip, which is also easy to untie. It is formed with two intertwined Overhand Knots (p.20), and can be tied in a wide range of material lines including bungee (shock) cord. Pull on both standing parts to tighten the knot.

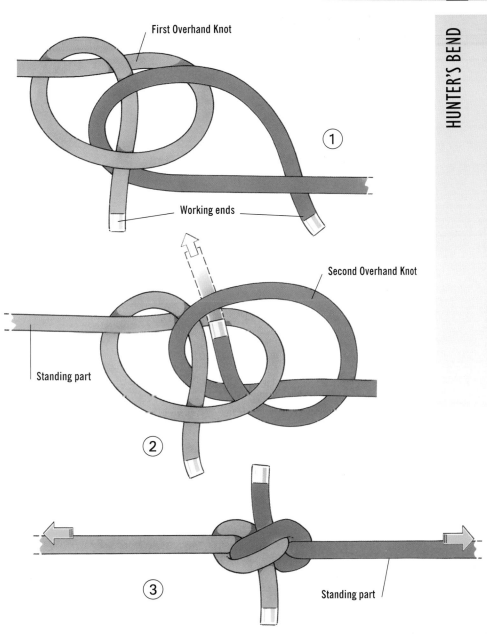

First Overhand Knot

Working ends

①

Second Overhand Knot

Standing part

②

③

Standing part

HARNESS BEND
Also known as: *Parcel Bend; Drawing Bend*

A practical knot, particularly suited to small line for parcel tying, or joining a broken lacing without having to unthread the whole lace. To tie, take the line under tension (if there is one) and make a loop as shown in step one. Pass the working end of the second rope through the loop and close it down. Now pass a Half Hitch (p.100) around the standing part and pull it down onto the loop.

 **TOP TIP**

Practice this knot with both an upward and a downward line under tension – it could be used either way

The Harness Bend has a number of practical uses

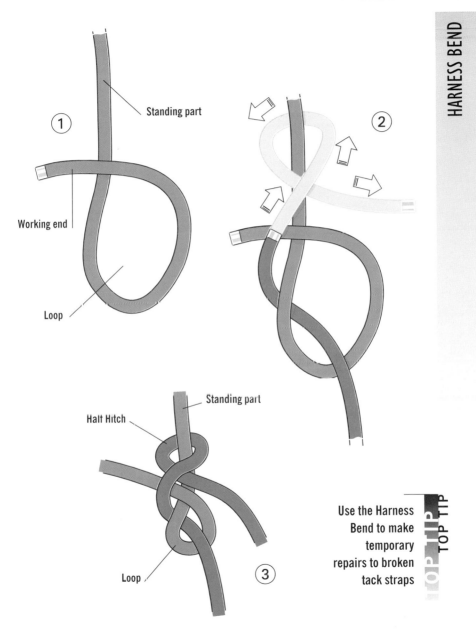

① Standing part

Working end

Loop

②

③

Standing part

Halt Hitch

Loop

BLOOD KNOT

Also known as: *Barrel Knot*

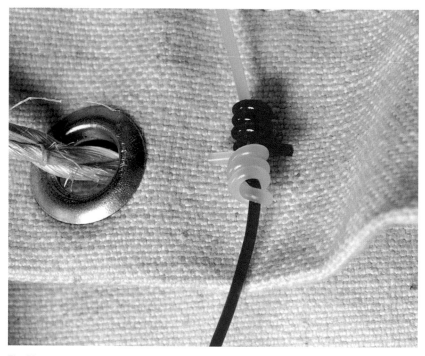

The Blood Knot tied in monofilament lines of similar thickness

TOP TIP

Before tying this knot, wet nylon line to make it more supple

The Blood Knot is perhaps the most popular of bends used by fishermen for joining two lines. It is particularly useful for joining nylon or monofilament lines where the standing part is either long or inaccessible, for instance, when on two spools.

Tie the Blood Knot using at least three tucks; a greater number will increase the strength of the knot. Once pulled up tight, however, this knot is virtually impossible to untie.

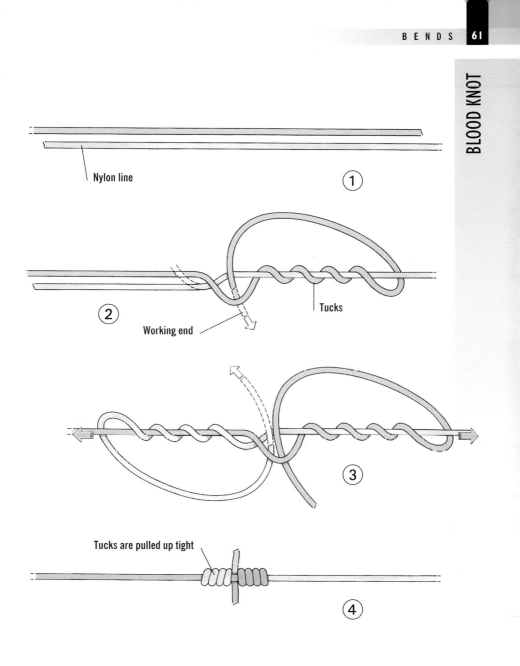

Nylon line

(1)

Tucks

Working end

(2)

(3)

Tucks are pulled up tight

(4)

WATER KNOT
Also known as: *Cove Knot*

The Water Knot tied in two lines of the same thickness

Ancient though this knot may be, it has stood the test of time in many different line materials, and still remains popular in the fishing world. One advantage of the Water Knot is that it can be tied in lines of differing thickness.

To tie, lay the two working ends parallel to one another (step one). Take the shorter line – or the line still on a spool – and position it on the inside of the loop (step two), ensuring that the loop is large enough to pass the right-hand standing part through. Form four tucks (step three), and pull up in the manner of the Multiple Overhand Knot (p.22).

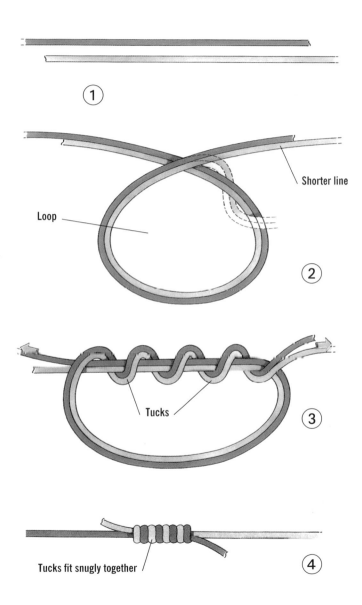

①

Shorter line

Loop

②

Tucks

③

Tucks fit snugly together

④

NAIL KNOT

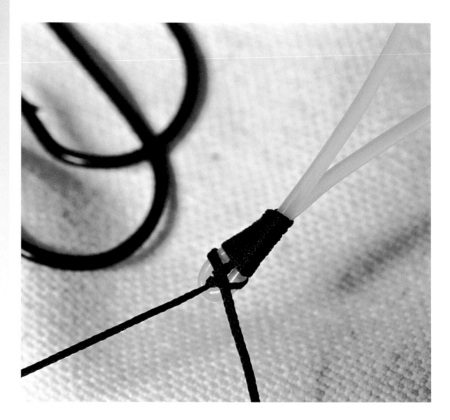

This method of tying a fly line to the braided backing is still favoured by some – despite the super-glued sleeve alternative – as it allows fly lines to be changed quickly and easily using the same backing and reel. Tie the Nail Knot with generous amounts of line both for security and ease of tying. Ensure that the working end of the backing line is trapped close into the bight of the line. Pull the turns up close to the bight.

Leave long ends when tying the Nail Knot

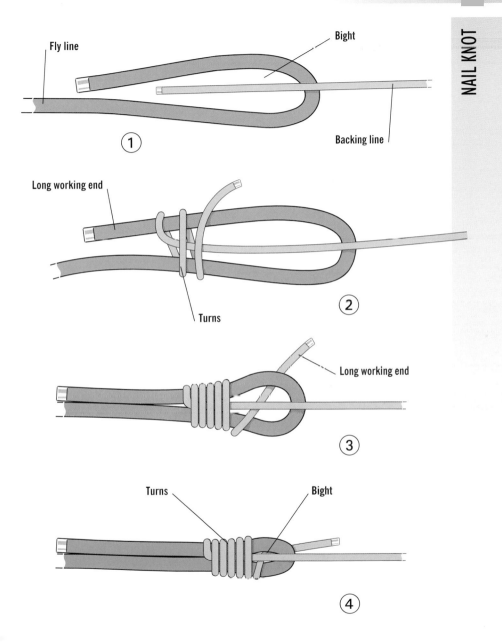

Fly line

Bight

Backing line

①

Long working end

Turns

②

Long working end

③

Turns

Bight

④

NEEDLE KNOT

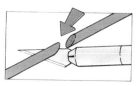

The Needle Knot is used to effect a smooth join between the fly line and the butt end of the leader. Not only is this an extremely strong method of fastening monofilament to fly line, but it is also unlikely to catch or snag as the line is fished.

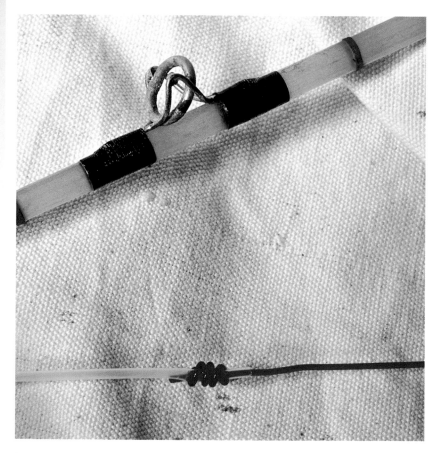

The Needle Knot forms a smooth join between fly line and leader

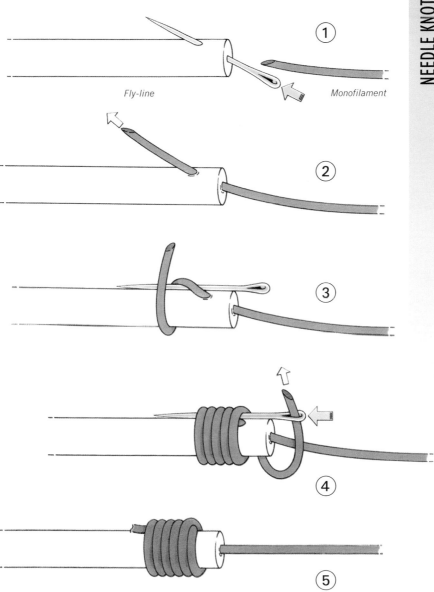

Fly-line   Monofilament

RACKING BEND

More secure than the Sheet Bend (p.44), the Racking Bend is used for tying a small diameter heaving line to a large hawser because it is necessary not only to attach the line, but to pull up and hold the bight formed in the end of the hawser. Use at least four turns and pull up each completed turn as tightly as possible before applying the next. Note that the Racking Bend is finished with a Half Hitch (p.100) around the standing part of the hawser.

The Racking Bend attaching a heaving line to a hawser

(1)

(2)

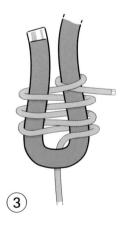

(3)

BOWLINE BEND

The Bowline Bend joins two ropes, irrespective of their relative size or material

Designed as an alternative to the Carrick Bend (p.52) for heavy hawsers, the Bowline Bend is used to join ropes of almost any thickness, in the knowledge that the Bowline is strong and can be untied even after it has been under strain. If necessary, the sharp bend formed by the two loops can be eased by "through footing" the second line to form a Reef Knot (p.72) at the join before tying the second Bowline.

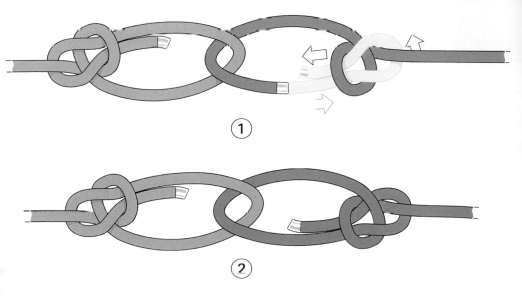

BINDING KNOTS

Binding knots usually employ both ends of the same line to bind, wrap or clamp other articles.

Uses for binding knots include:

To tie the ends of a bandage or triangular bandage sling; to tie sail reef points; to tie back tent doors and walls with tapes –
Reef Knot (p.72)

To tie slippery line around a bundle or object –
Surgeon's Knot (p.74)

To grip, stop or temporarily whip the end of a rope –
Constrictor Knot (p.76)

To lash together a bundle; to lash a sail to a spar or boom –
Marline Hitch (p 78)

To support a scaffolding plank; to lash together sticks, poles, planks –
Oklahoma Hitch (p.80)

To lash small-diameter bamboo etc. at right angles –
Transom Knot (p.82)

To tie a noose around a parcel –
Packer's Knot (p.83)

To lash two poles at right angles –
Square Lashing (p.84)

To make a Sheer Legs with two poles –
Sheer Lashing (p.86)

To make a diagonal brace for frameworks –
Diagonal Lashing (p.88)

To whip the ends of laid or braided matt or hairy ropes –
Common Whipping (p.90)
French Whipping (p.91)

To whip or bind any part of a rope –
West Country Whipping (p.92)

To whip the end of laid natural or man-made fibre rope –
Sailmaker's Whipping (p.94)

REEF KNOT
Also known as: *Square Knot*

"The Reef Knot is designed to join together two lines of equal thickness". Oh how that statement has perpetuated the wrongful use of this knot by so many of us in the past. Yes, it is designed to join the ends of line together, and a very handsome and flat knot it makes, but only if used for the right purpose. The reef points of a sail are secured by tying their ends around the boom or yard (which is where the name originates). A triangular or strip bandage has two ends which can be very neatly tied with a knot that lies flat and comfortable; many other soft materials can also be bound with this knot tied in the two ends of a piece of line.

This knot should not be used as a bend. It is unsafe and, should it capsize, will form a Lark's Head Knot around one line, through which that line can easily slip. The Reef Knot is used extensively in macramé when it is known as the Square Knot.

A Reef Knot tied in the ends of a cord binding a roll of soft material

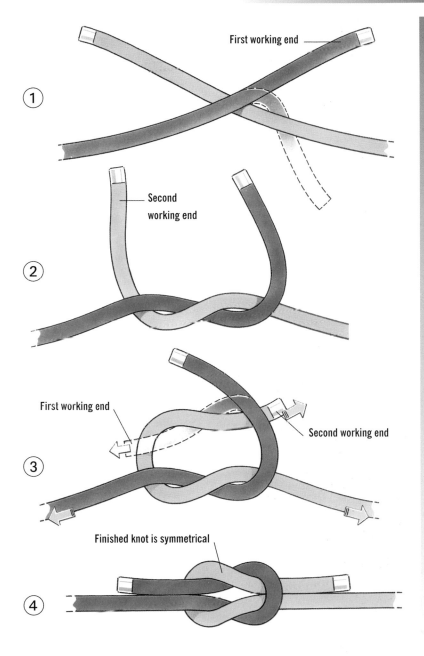

First working end

Second working end

First working end

Second working end

Finished knot is symmetrical

(1)

(2)

(3)

(4)

SURGEON'S KNOT

Used to tie off the ends of slippery material, this knot is used by surgeons to tie off blood vessels, but it is equally at home in nylon, monofilament and other slippery materials. It can be used as a binding knot, with an equal number of tucks top and bottom (right) or a bend, which is best tied with two primary tucks and one secondary tuck (opposite). Pull on the standing parts to tighten the knot.

The Surgeon's Knot tied in mono-filament line so that it lies flat

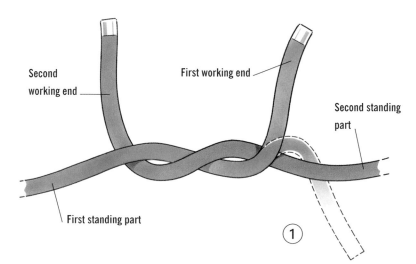

Second working end

First working end

Second standing part

First standing part

1

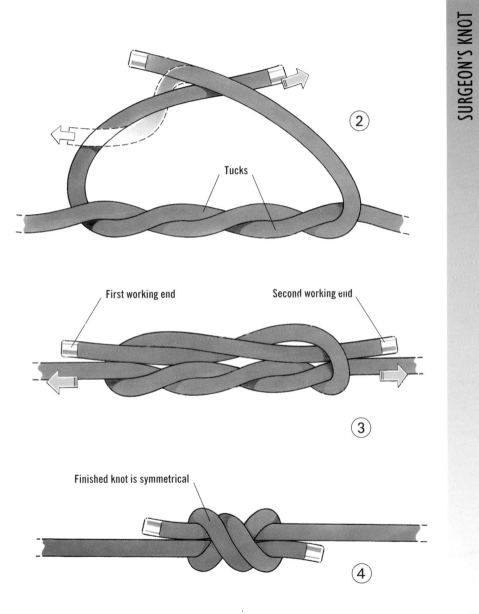

(2)

Tucks

First working end   Second working end

(3)

Finished knot is symmetrical

(4)

CONSTRICTOR KNOT

The Constrictor Knot as a temporary whipping or stop at the end of a rope

More a tool than merely a knot, the Constrictor Knot has perhaps more uses than any other single knot and should rank high on your list of knots to learn, no matter what your following. Among its uses are: the temporary whipping on the end of a rope or at the throat of a splice; a grip around a bundle of lines; a clamp to hold projects being glued and for general use as a third hand.

The knot is formed in the same way as the Clove Hitch (p.106), but the working end is tucked under the lower crossing turn to form an Overhand Knot (p.20), which is trapped securely when pulled up. The knot stays tied and grips firmly so, in most cases, will be impossible to untie. Therefore, should you use it to secure an article, such as the neck of a sack, it will be prudent to make the tucked end a slipped one.

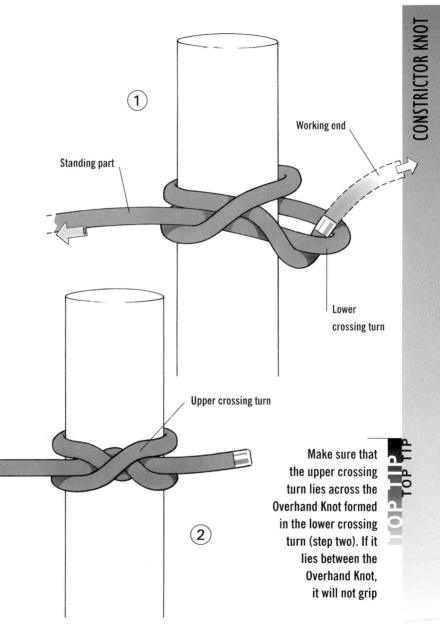

①

Standing part

Working end

Lower crossing turn

Upper crossing turn

②

Make sure that the upper crossing turn lies across the Overhand Knot formed in the lower crossing turn (step two). If it lies between the Overhand Knot, it will not grip

MARLINE HITCH

The Marline Hitch has a variety of uses, including lashing for a hammock and to drag a log or spar

The Marline Hitch is really an "in between" lashing. It can only be tied in a line that has been secured to an object by another knot – the Timber Hitch (p.101) – or through an Eye Splice (p.190), and has to be secured at the end with a Clove Hitch (p.106) or a Half Hitch (p.100).

The advantage of the Marline Hitch over the Half Hitch is that, because the working end goes first over then under the standing part, it tightens down better. By forming the hitch, pulling the line down and away from you, and then heaving it back to a central position (more than once if necessary), when tight, it will hold while the next tuck is made. Use this knot for lashing up a hammock, to secure long bundles or with a Timber Hitch to pull a log or spar, end first.

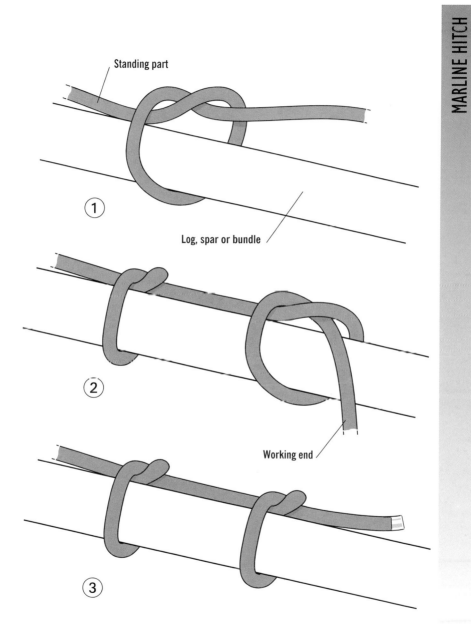

Standing part

① Log, spar or bundle

② Working end

③

OKLAHOMA HITCH

Also known as: *Scaffold Hitch; Pole Lashing*

The Oklahoma Hitch
used to suspend a
scaffolding plank

Use this knot to clamp articles together while fixing or gluing takes place

As its alternative names suggest, the Oklahoma Hitch can be used for a number of applications. A scaffolding plank can be supported with this knot at each end. When tied, bring the ends of the rope up and tie the working end to the standing part with a Bowline (p.156) as shown above. To use it as a lashing around sticks, poles, emergency fracture splints and so on, pull the ends tight then tie off using a Reef Knot (p.72).

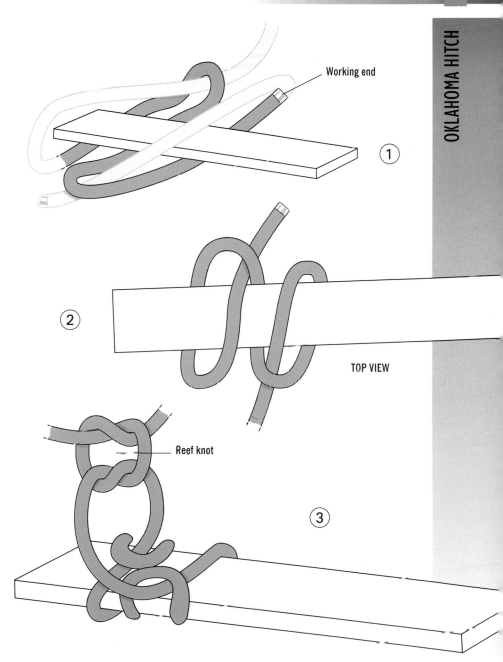

Working end

①

② TOP VIEW

Reef knot

③

TRANSOM KNOT

The Transom Knot makes a secure binding for garden canes

Similar to the Constrictor Knot (p.76), the Transom Knot provides a binding that holds well and can be difficult or even impossible to untie. Useful as a temporary square lashing, the join can be strengthened by tying the same knot on the reverse of the cross members. Commonly used to secure garden canes or trellis work. Like the Constrictor Knot, the ends of the Transom Knot can be cut off close up to the knot for a neat finish.

① ②

PACKER'S KNOT

The Packer's Knot is often used to tie parcels

The Packer's Knot is a handy device for pulling a line taut around an object, and gripping it while you make the next turn or secure it with a Half Hitch (p.100). When tied around an object, pull the standing part and the knot tightens and holds it in place; pull the tail of the knot and the standing part is released. This handy practical application of the Figure-of-Eight Knot (p.26) is commonly used for tying parcels, bundles, rolled meat joints and the neck of a sack which needs to be opened and closed frequently. A stopper knot can be used on the working end of the Figure-of-Eight Knot for added security.

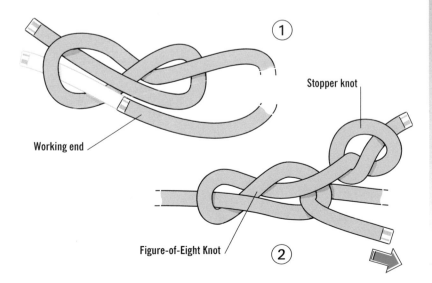

①

Working end

Stopper knot

Figure-of-Eight Knot

②

SQUARE LASHING

The Square Lashing – joining two poles at right angles as part of a framework

The Square Lashing is used to lash together two poles at right angles, normally as part of a structure such as scaffolding or a square frame. Start with a Clove Hitch (p.106) around the upright, twisting the tail around the line (step one). Make sure that each turn is pulled up tight (use a lever if possible) before the next is applied. Three or four turns should be sufficient with two or three frapping turns. Finish off with a Clove Hitch, applying the first Half Hitch with its entry as close to the frapping turns as possible.

TOP TIP

When building a frame, make a temporary construction using the Transom Knot (p.82) to hold the poles in place

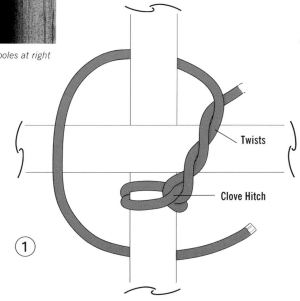

Twists

Clove Hitch

①

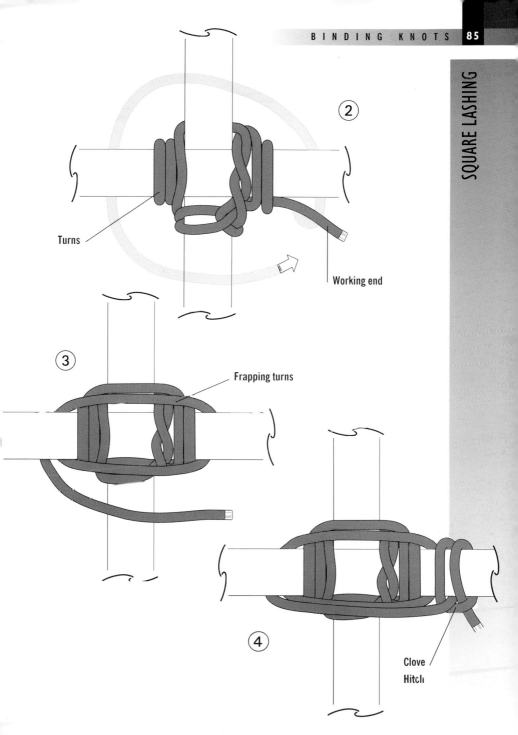

②

Turns

Working end

③

Frapping turns

④

Clove
Hitch

SHEER LASHING

Sheer Lashing can be used either to
form a joint at the top of two poles so
that the legs can be splayed to form
Sheer Legs, or to lash two poles parallel
to each other to extend their length.

The number of turns required will
depend on the thickness of the poles.
As a rough guide, the width of the
lashing should be not less than the
combined width of the two poles.
When applying the turns lay them
neatly, but not tight, then add at least
two frapping turns between the poles.
Finish the lashing with a Clove Hitch
(p.106), making sure that the first half
hitch has its entry as close to the
frapping turns as possible. To stop the
legs from splaying while in use, tie a
brace between the two legs about 30cm
(12in) from the bottom, using a Clove
Hitch to secure each end to the legs.

Sheer Lashing, joining two spars to form sheer legs

*When extending the
length of a pole, use two
Sheer Lashings without
frapping turns. Heave
each turn up as tightly
as possible, then hammer
wedges between the
poles and the lashing
to tighten (right)*

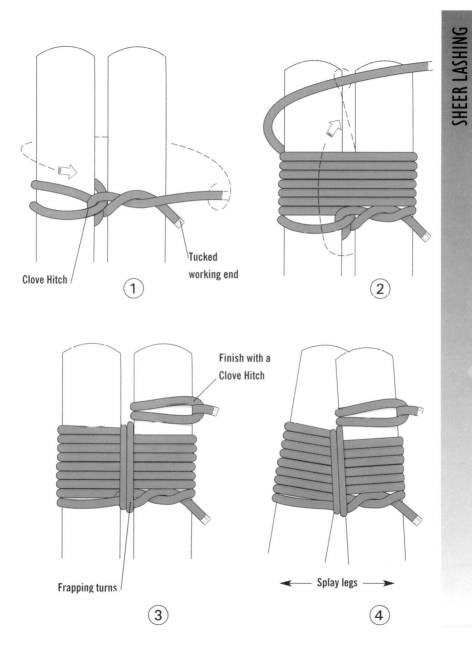

Clove Hitch

Tucked working end

(1)

(2)

Frapping turns

Finish with a Clove Hitch

(3)

◄── Splay legs ──►

(4)

DIAGONAL LASHING

The Diagonal Lashing is designed to hold cross bracing poles in place. Start with a Timber Hitch (p.101) through the largest opening, and continue with three or four binding turns in each direction, pulling each one as tight as possible before applying the next. Finish off with a Clove Hitch (p.106), applying the first half hitch with its entry as close to the frapping turns as possible.

The Diagonal Lashing at the centre crossing of bracing poles

TOP TIP

A heaving board, hammer or axe handle can be used as a lever to pull turns up tight. Take two or three turns around the handle, wedge the head against one of the poles and heave the line up tight

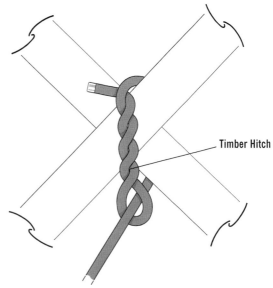

①

Timber Hitch

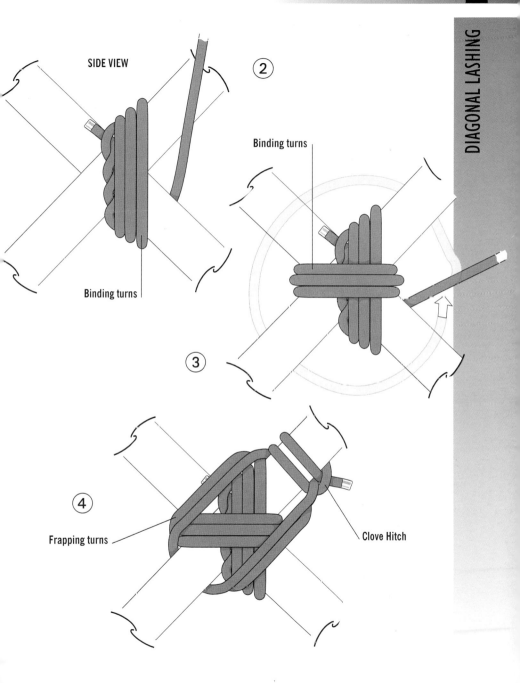

SIDE VIEW

②

Binding turns

Binding turns

③

④

Frapping turns

Clove Hitch

COMMON WHIPPING

The Common Whipping using waxed twine on natural fibre rope

The Common Whipping is quick and simple to apply. It is most effective if applied in waxed whipping twine, a short distance from the end of a rope. The whipping should be as tight as possible, and be about one to one and a half times the diameter of the rope. Use on natural fibre and braided synthetics, but only as a temporary whipping on stranded nylon or polypropylene as it easily slips off.

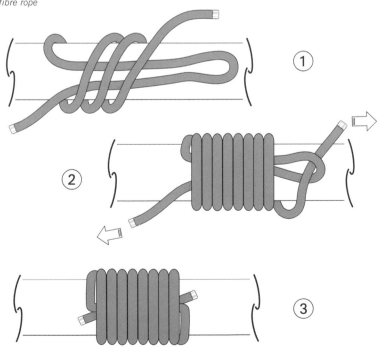

FRENCH WHIPPING

French Whipping differs
from Common Whipping in
that it consists of a series of
Half Hitches (p.100),
resulting in an attractive spiral
design. As with the Common
Whipping (p.90), the French
Whipping should be between
one and one and a half times
the diameter of the rope,
and works most effectively
on natural fibre and braided
synthetic ropes.

The French Whipping is tied with a series of Half Hitches

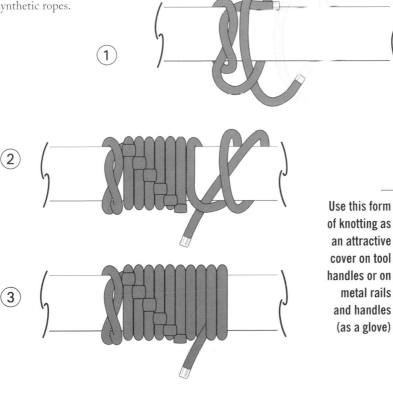

1

2

3

WEST COUNTRY WHIPPING

West Country Whipping is formed by tying a series of Overhand Knots (p.20) around a rope on alternate sides. As with other whippings, the West Country Whipping is most effective when applied in waxed whipping twine, a short distance from the end of a rope. However, because of the way it is tied, this whipping is useful on any part of a rope.

It should be between one and one and a half times the diameter of the rope in length. Form the Overhand Knots as tightly as possible and finish with a Reef Knot (p.72). Use this whipping on natural fibre and braided synthetics, but only as a temporary whipping on stranded nylon or poly-propylene as it can slip off.

The West Country Whipping, applied in waxed whipping twine a short distance from the end of a rope

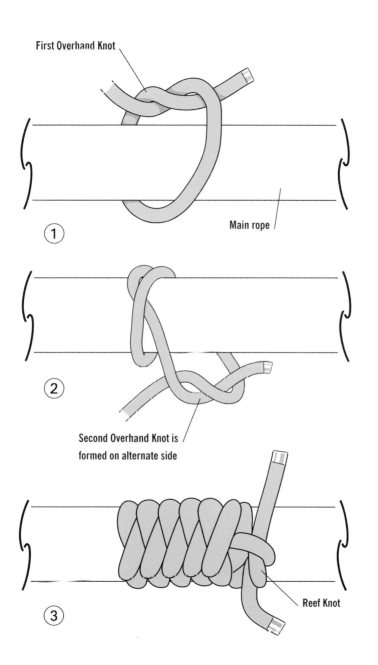

First Overhand Knot

Main rope

(1)

(2)

Second Overhand Knot is
formed on alternate side

Reef Knot

(3)

SAILMAKER'S WHIPPING

Sailmaker's Whipping is perhaps the best permanent whipping for the end of any stranded rope. As with other whippings, it is most effective when applied in waxed whipping twine, a short distance from the end of the rope. The whipping should be as tight as possible, between one and one and a half times the diameter of the rope in length and finished with a Reef Knot (p.72) between the strands. Use this whipping on natural fibre and synthetic stranded rope.

The Sailmaker's Whipping tied on stranded rope

TOP TIP

When finishing, pull up tightly so that the Reef Knot beds securely between the strand ends

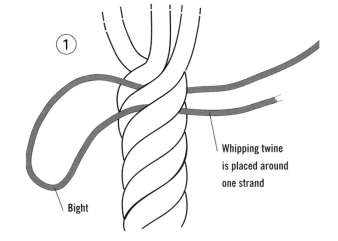

Whipping twine is placed around one strand

Bight

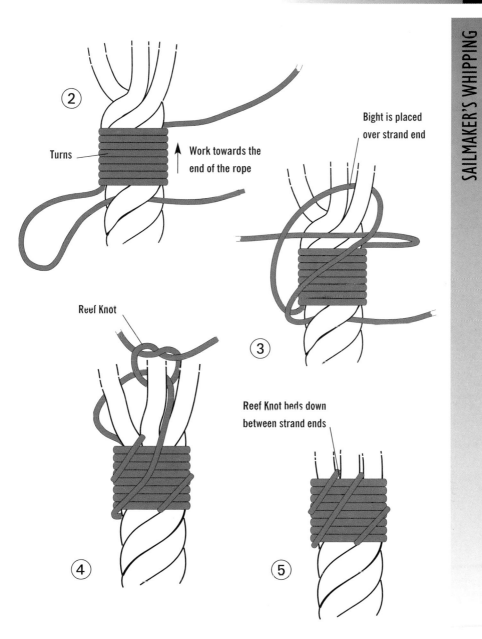

(2)

Turns

Work towards the
end of the rope

Bight is placed
over strand end

(3)

Reef Knot

Reef Knot beds down
between strand ends

(4)

(5)

SEIZING

Flat Seizing – used to lash together two parts of the same rope

When two ropes or two parts of a rope are "married" then bound together, the binding is called Seizing. The Flat Seizing (opposite and above) is started with the working end of the line being passed through a spliced eye. This draws the two ropes together before the binding takes place; a Timber Hitch (p.101) will suffice if the material cannot be spliced. The length of Seizing is dependent on the application, but should be not less than the combined width of the two ropes.

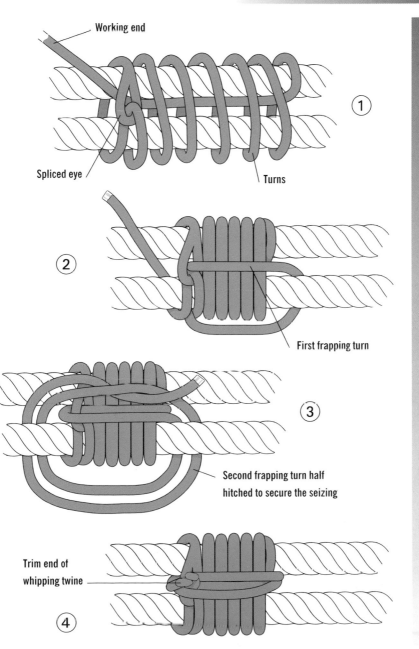

Working end

Spliced eye

Turns

1

First frapping turn

2

Second frapping turn half
hitched to secure the seizing

3

Trim end of
whipping twine

4

HITCHES

A "Hitch" is used to attach a rope to a rail, spar, jackstay, handrail, ring, tool handle, post, bollard, hook, swivel, karabiner or another rope.

Uses for hitches include:

For added security to knots –
Half Hitch (p.100)

To attach the start of a lashing or attachment knot to a log or spar –
Timber Hitch (p.101)

To attach a lead to a stake –
Cow Hitch (p.102)

To attach a loop to a ring –
Ring Hitch (p.104)

To attach a sling to a lifting hook –
Cat's Paw (p.105)

To attach a rope to a horizontal spar or other rope –
Clove Hitch (p.106)

To secure a rope to a ring or pole –
Round Turn & Two Half Hitches (p.110)

To secure a towing line to a log or spar –
Rolling Hitch (p.114)

To secure a line to any cylindrical object for lifting or towing –
Icicle Hitch (p.116)

To tether an animal to a ring or pole –
Halter Hitch (p.118)
Highwayman's Hitch (p.120)

To secure the painter of a small boat to a bollard, post or stake –
Mooring Hitch (p.122)

To hoist or lower a sealed barrel or drum –
Barrel Hitch (p.124)

To attach a vertically adjustable strop and karabiner to a rope –
Bachmann Knot (p.126)

To attach a strop to vertical or horizontal rope –
Prusik Knot (p.128)

To pay out a rope under control –
Italian Hitch (p.130)

HALF HITCH

Although the Half Hitch is a knot in its own right, it is rarely used alone. Tied around a spar or ring, it will only hold successfully if the rope is not slippery. More often than not, the Half Hitch is used in a supporting role, for instance, to hold the round turn in place in the Round Turn and Two Half Hitches (p.110). Combining two Half Hitches results in knots such as the Cow Hitch (p.102) and Clove Hitch (p.106). A series of Half Hitches is used to form a French Whipping (p.91) at the end of a rope, or the handsome Cockscombing (p.214), which is used as a handgrip and decorative cover on rails or rings.

A single turn supported with a Half Hitch

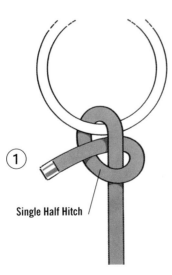

(1)

Single Half Hitch

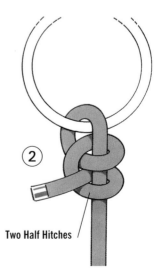

(2)

Two Half Hitches

TIMBER HITCH

The Timber Hitch is quick to tie, never jams and is easy to untie, making it a convenient way of securing a rope around a cylindrical object, particularly when the end must be anchored to support another knot or lashing. Used together with one or two Half Hitches (p.100), the Timber Hitch secures a rope that can be used to hoist a cylindrical object, or drag it over the ground or through water. Take care to tie this knot correctly. Pass a fairly long working end around the object, take it around the standing part and then tuck the working end back around itself (with the lay of the rope, if it is stranded) for at least 3 tucks – or more if the circumference of the object will allow.

The Timber Hitch secures a rope around a log, enabling it to be dragged

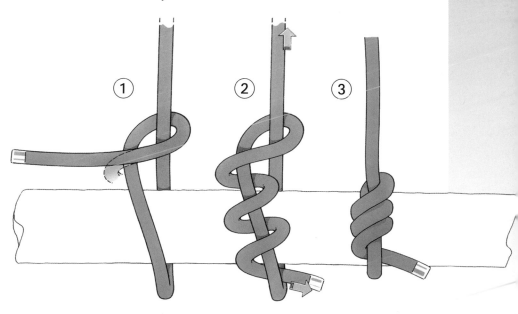

① ② ③

COW HITCH

Also known as: *Ring Hitch; Lark's Head; Girth Knot*

This versatile knot takes the form of two opposite hitches over the standing part of another rope structure, through a ring or around a rail or post. It is used extensively to commence macramé projects and also is useful for suspending objects with loop handles from hooks, rings or lines. It can be tied using four methods.

For the first method, pass the working end around the object and pull up before applying the second hitch. Because the load is applied only to the standing part,

the working end may then need to be secured, either by a Half Hitch (p.100) or Seizing (p.96) around the standing part. Alternatively, the working end can be passed between the bight and the object to form a Pedigree Cow Hitch (left).

To tie the Cow Hitch using the second method, feed the bight over or through the object – such as a clasp knife or Lanyard Loop – and pass the two ends through the bight.

For the third method, pass the bight of a closed loop – such as a baggage label tie – through a ring, then pass the object attached to the loop through the bight.

The fourth method involves passing the end of a leather or webbing strap through a ring to make the first hitch. Then pass the second hitch so that the end lays on top of the standing part and is pulled up to look like a necktie.

The Pedigree Cow Hitch (left) is a variation of the Cow Hitch. The working end has been tucked back under the bight for added security

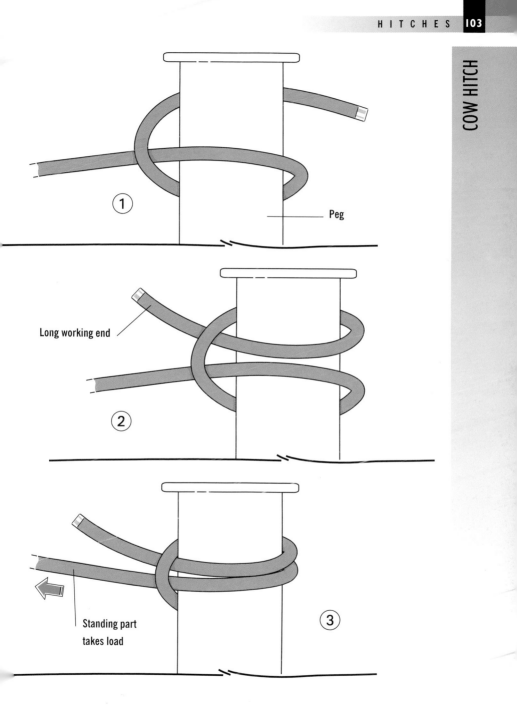

① Peg

② Long working end

③ Standing part takes load

RING HITCH

The Ring Hitch is used to attach a ring to a soft eye, a Lanyard Loop (p.176) or a bight. It is most commonly used where either the ring or the line can be passed through to form what are essentially two Half Hitches (p.100) on a ring. The Ring Hitch can also be tied by passing one end of a line through a ring (below).

The bights of hammock nettles secured to a ring with Ring Hitches (left)

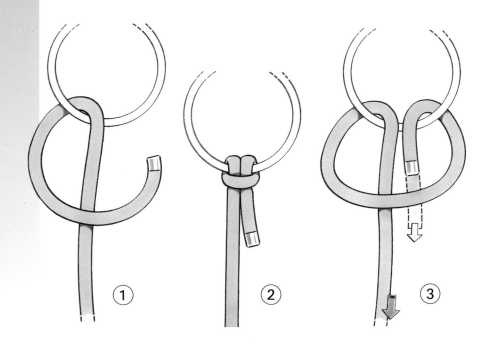

① ② ③

CAT'S PAW

This is the best way to attach a strop or loop to a hook as the strain is taken equally on both sides. When a loaded strop is passed over the bill of a hook, the safe working load of the line is considerably reduced. This is because the rope fibres nearest the hook are being pulled at an acute angle, putting most of the load on the outer fibres. The advantage of using the Cat's Paw is that in the event of one leg breaking, the other will hold long enough to lower the load safely.

The Cat's Paw under load

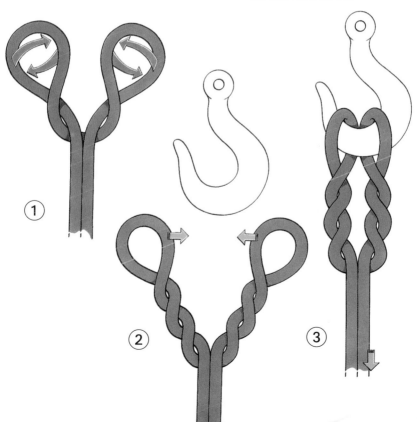

CLOVE HITCH

An everyday, useful and easy-to-tie knot, the Clove Hitch is a good binding knot. As a hitch, however, it should be used with caution as it may come undone if the object around which it is tied can rotate, or if constant pressure is not maintained on one or both ends of the rope. This particularly applies to slippery man-made-fibre ropes such as polypropylene. In practical terms there are two methods of tying the Clove Hitch: method one is shown opposite; method two on p.108.

The Slipped Clove Hitch is a convenient way of temporarily tethering an animal lead, the inboard end of a heaving line to a guard rail, or tying the neck of a sack.

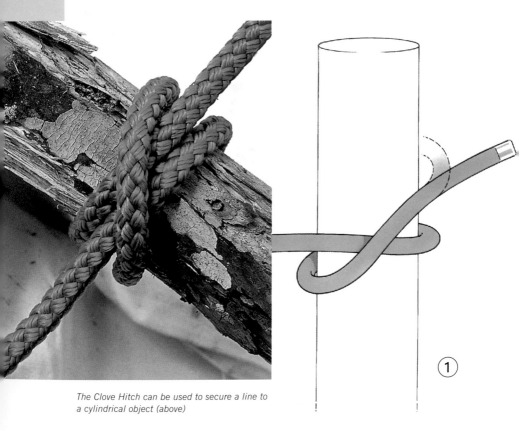

The Clove Hitch can be used to secure a line to a cylindrical object (above)

①

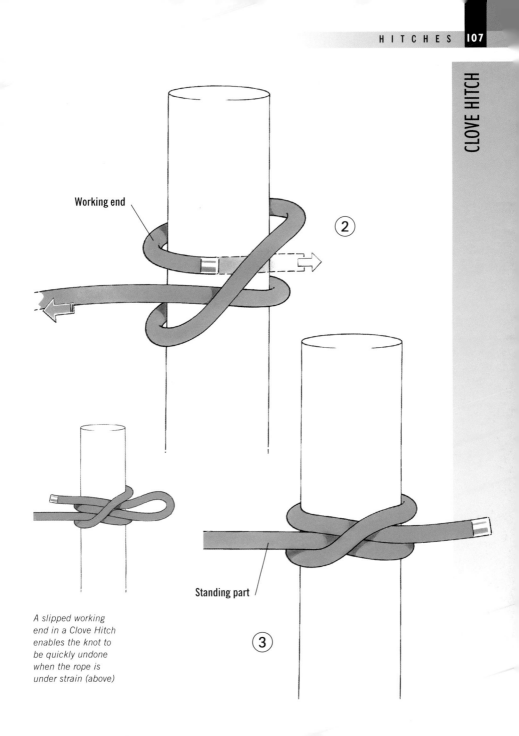

Working end

②

Standing part

③

A slipped working end in a Clove Hitch enables the knot to be quickly undone when the rope is under strain (above)

CLOVE HITCH (POST)

When the end of a post, rail or bollard is accessible, the Clove Hitch can be tied using two Half Hitches (p.100). These can be pre-formed and dropped over the end of the post (below) or, particularly if the line needs to be pulled taut, placed over the post one at a time.

The Clove Hitch made with two Half Hitches and dropped over a bollard

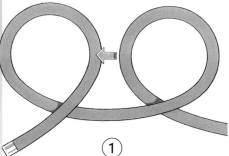

①

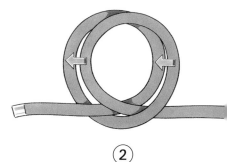

②

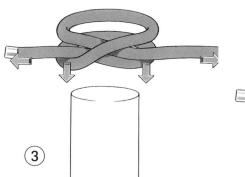

③

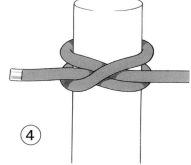

④

CLOVE HITCH (POST)

CLOVE HITCH (RING)

The Clove Hitch can also be used to make a line fast to a ring. It is easy to adjust when the weight is off the line, so is particularly useful if the length of line needs to be regulated. Leave a long working end so that it will not pull through the knot. Alternatively, seize, tape or Half Hitch (p.100) the working end to the standing part.

The Clove Hitch making fast a line to a ring

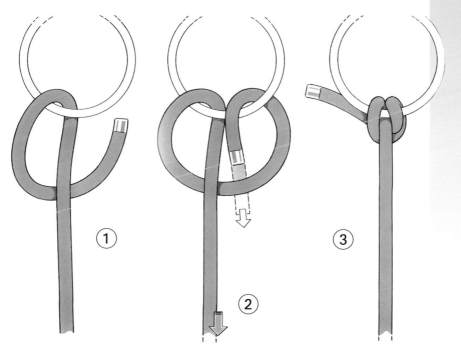

ROUND TURN & TWO HALF HITCHES

Like the Fisherman's Bend (p.112), this knot is strong, dependable and used to attach a line to a ring, post or rail. Easy to learn and tie, it is probably one of the most useful knots in regular use today.

A round turn passed around a static object will support a considerable load, provided that the working end is held in hand or, as with this knot, secured with two half hitches. If the load cannot be held easily, make one or two more turns before applying the half hitches.

The many uses for this knot include: to attach a swing rope to a tree branch or frame; to attach the painter of a small craft to a mooring ring or rail; and to attach a tow rope to a vehicle. For added security, tape or seize the working end to the standing part after the knot has been drawn up tight.

The Round Turn & Two Half Hitches – a multi-purpose and commonly used knot

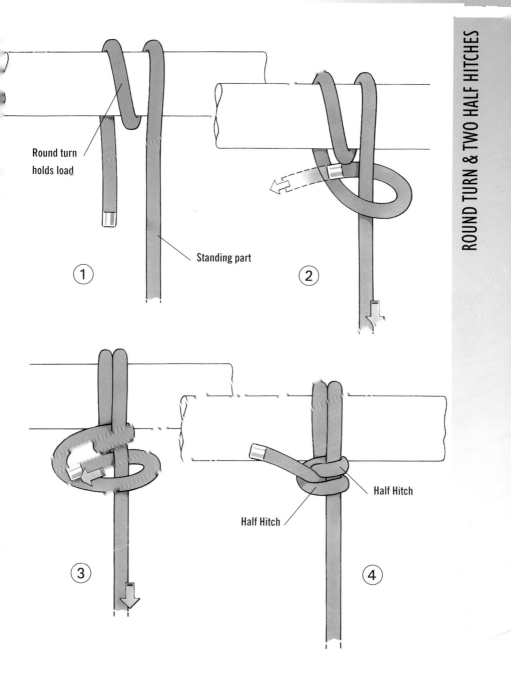

Round turn holds load

Standing part

① ② ③ ④

Half Hitch

Half Hitch

FISHERMAN'S BEND

Also known as: *Anchor Bend*

This hitch is a stable and reliable knot for use in almost any type or size of rope, cord or line. It can be used to attach rope to an anchor, moor a boat to a ring, attach monofilament line to a swivel or attach a lead rope to a harness ring. For added security, tie a Half Hitch (p.100) around the standing part of the rope or line. For a more permanent arrangement, seize the working end to the standing part.

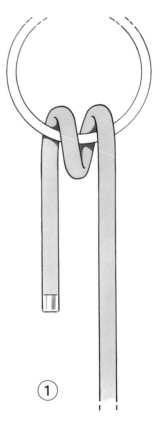

(1)

The Fisherman's Bend with an added Half Hitch

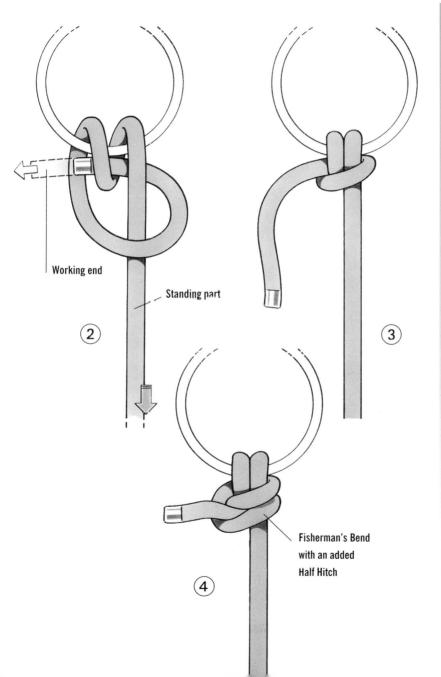

Working end

Standing part

②

③

④

Fisherman's Bend
with an added
Half Hitch

ROLLING HITCH
Also known as: *Magnus Hitch; Taut-line Hitch*

Where a lengthways pull from a pole or static line is needed, this old faithful takes some beating. Three ways of tying this hitch have evolved over the years.

The first, for use around a pole, is commenced by passing two round turns around the pole, crossing those with the working end and adding a Half Hitch (p.100) on the opposite side to the line of pull (opposite).

Use the second method for attaching a light line to a rope or cable. Make one turn around the pole, add a riding turn and complete with a Half Hitch as with the first method.

The third method – also known as the Taut-line Hitch method – may be tied with the working end emerging from the final Half Hitch and parallel with the standing part (far right).

A Rolling Hitch with riding turns, normally used on a large rope or cable

ROLLING HITCH

Round turn

①

Direction of pull or load

②

Working end

③

Leave a long
working end

The Taut-line Hitch (above)

ICICLE HITCH

The Icicle Hitch – a more secure alternative to the Rolling Hitch and the Timber Hitch

There are times when the Rolling Hitch (p.114) or a Timber Hitch (p.101) and Half Hitch (p.100) just will not hold, especially on smooth surfaces; in all but the rare frictionless circumstances, the Icicle Hitch will. John Smith revealed this knot at a meeting of the International Guild of Knot Tyers (IGKT), where he suspended his weight on a line – tied using the Icicle Hitch – to a smooth wooden fid, point down. High on my inventory of useful practical knots, the Icicle Hitch can be used to pull plastic hose, wires or swabs through conduits and ducting, or hoist cylindrical objects, such as scaffold poles or masts. Do *not* be tempted to use supporting Half Hitches in front of the Icicle Hitch as it needs a direct pull.

TOP TIP

Place the knot under full pressure and let it grip properly before use

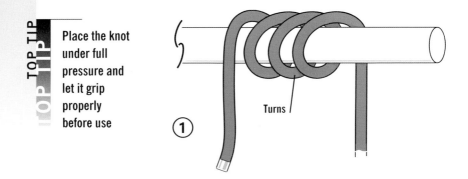

Turns

(1)

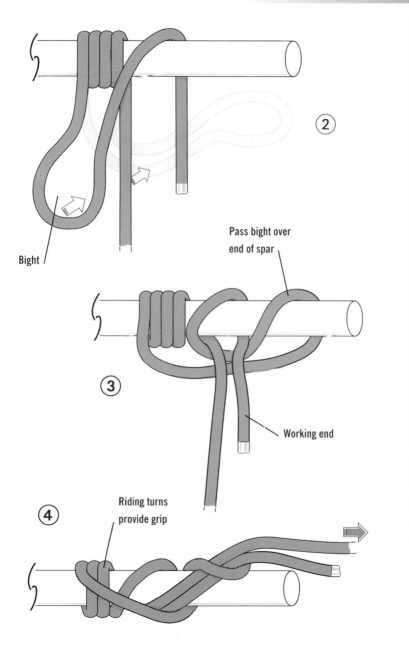

Bight

Pass bight over
end of spar

②

③ Working end

④ Riding turns
provide grip

HALTER HITCH

The Halter Hitch is a form of Overhand Noose, with the Overhand Knot slipped. This makes it a useful general purpose hitch particularly suited to tethering animals, because no matter how much strain is applied to the halter or lead rope, the Slipped Overhand Knot (p.21) can still be undone. To stop the animal inadvertently slipping the knot, pass the working end through the slipped loop (step two). Pull on the standing part to tighten the knot.

This knot can be tied with reins, using the bight as a working end

A loosely formed Halter Hitch is sufficient to secure a tame animal and easier to untie

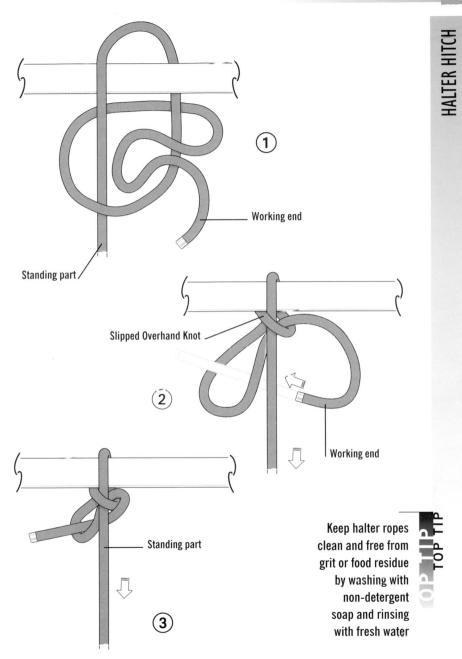

① Working end

Standing part

Slipped Overhand Knot

② Working end

③ Standing part

HIGHWAYMAN'S HITCH

Also known as: *Draw Hitch*

This hitch is useful for securing a line to a rail or spar, especially if the rope needs to be recovered from out of reach or released quickly. The standing part of the hitch takes the load and the working end is slipped, such that when it is pulled the rope is released from the fixture. Use the Highwayman's Hitch as a temporary mooring for a small boat or for tethering an animal, but remember that it can be released inadvertently, or by animals that like to chew on the ends of rope!

The Highwayman's Hitch is not considered safe for human descent purposes.

The Highwayman's Hitch on a rail (opposite)

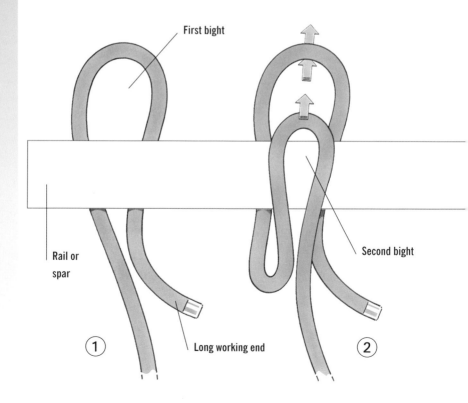

First bight

Rail or spar

Long working end

Second bight

(1)   (2)

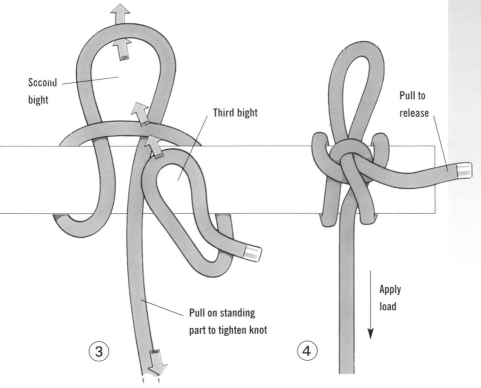

Second bight

Third bight

Pull to release

Pull on standing part to tighten knot

Apply load

③

④

MOORING HITCH

There are a multitude of Mooring Hitches, and this is but one variation used to moor a vessel to a bollard. The important feature of this method is that it uses two (or more) round turns to hold the load and therefore only needs minimal force to hold the turns to prevent slipping. Quick and easy to apply by one person, it is also easy to release or pay-out a little at a time, if necessary, in a tideway.

A Mooring Hitch secured with a Half Hitch

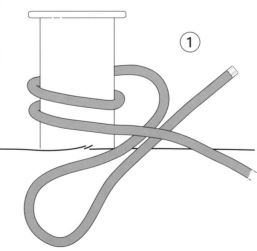

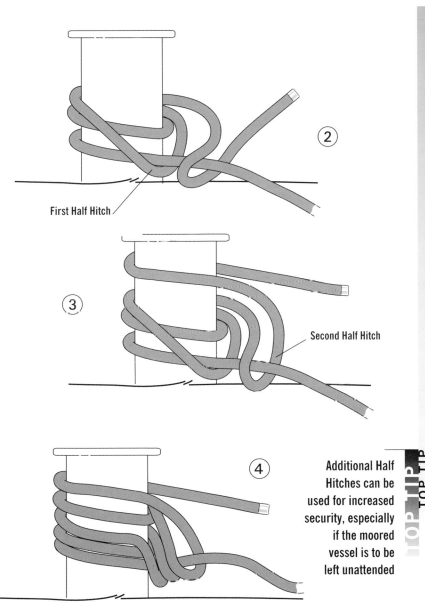

First Half Hitch

②

③

Second Half Hitch

④

Additional Half Hitches can be used for increased security, especially if the moored vessel is to be left unattended

TOP TIP

BARREL HITCH

This method of slinging a barrel or drum with sealed ends employs a ready-made rope or webbing strop. Alternatively, a strop can be made by joining the ends of a short piece of rope with a Fisherman's Knot (p.47). Make sure that the strop is well splayed out under the barrel by taking up the slack and adjusting it before hoisting or lowering.

TOP TIP

For added security, twist a Cat's Paw (p.105) into the strop before attaching to a hook

The Barrel Hitch – used to hoist and lower a load

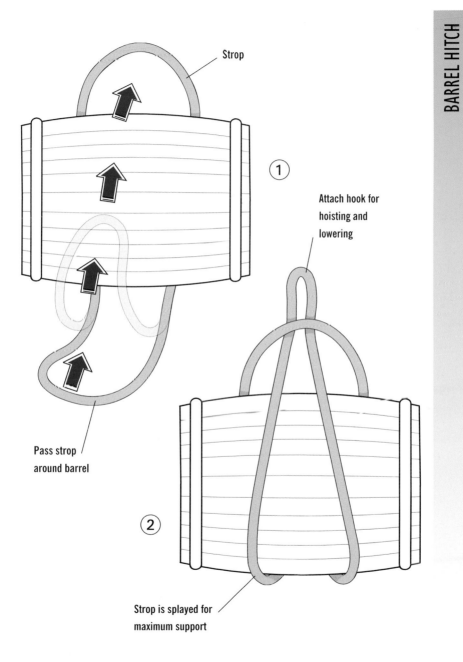

Strop

Attach hook for
hoisting and
lowering

①

Pass strop
around barrel

②

Strop is splayed for
maximum support

BACHMANN KNOT

Used primarily by cavers and climbers, the Bachmann Knot is designed as a vertically adjustable strop that can be used to support a person or equipment under load.

Start by making a temporary strop, which should be made from rope not more than half the diameter of the vertical rope and joined with a Fisherman's Knot (p.47). Clip the strop into the karabiner and make three or more turns around the vertical rope, keeping any join in the strop away from the turns.

The load is supported by the strop binding on the vertical rope; when the load is released the strop can be moved, using the karabiner as a handle.

Do not use this knot to support a person without proper supervision or instruction from a qualified climbing, caving or industrial roping instructor.

The Bachmann Knot, tied using a temporary strop joined with a Fisherman's Knot (p.47)

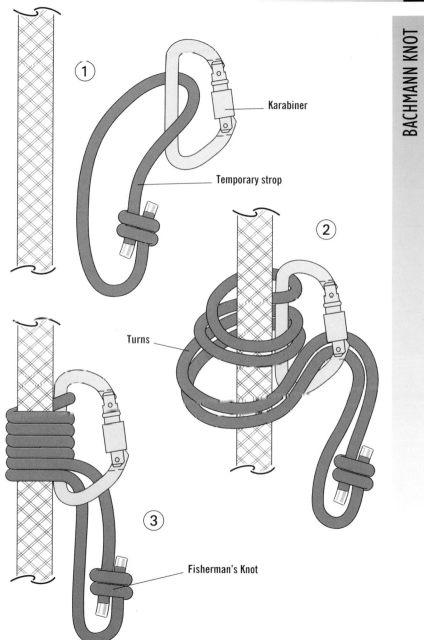

① Karabiner

Temporary strop

②

Turns

③

Fisherman's Knot

PRUSIK KNOT

This is one method of attaching a sling strop to a vertical or horizontal rope. The line used for the sling should be no more than half the diameter of the main rope.

Form a Lark's Head with the bight of the strop, then apply at least two turns with the outer bight. More turns will, of course, increase the grip of the knot, but only if the turns lay snug against the main rope with no overriding turns. When weight is applied to the sling, the turns grip against the rope. Releasing the load allows the hitch to be moved up, down or along the rope.

The Prusik Knot can be used on vertical or horizontal rope spans

TOP TIP

Use the Fisherman's Knot to make a loop, but ensure that the join is positioned away from the Prusik Knot

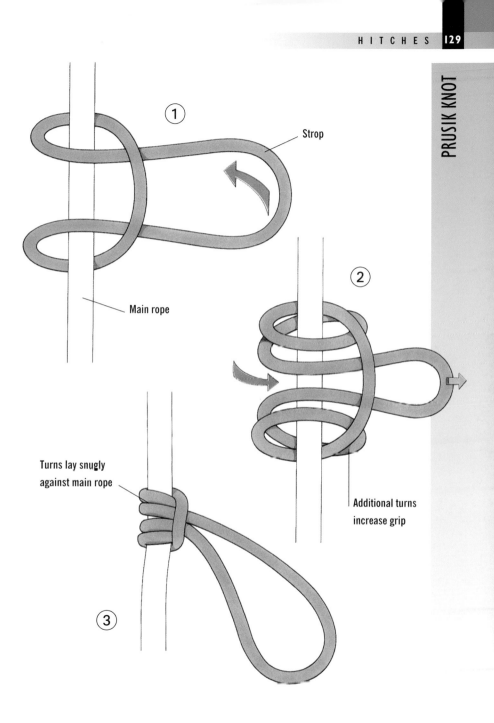

① Strop

Main rope

②

Additional turns
increase grip

Turns lay snugly
against main rope

③

ITALIAN HITCH

Also known as: *Munter Friction Hitch; Sliding Ring Hitch*

The Italian Hitch reversed, changing the role of each line

Essentially a climber's hitch, the Italian Hitch is designed to allow a loaded rope or line to be "paid out" under the control of a working end, which is used as a brake. If, while not under load, the working end is pulled so that the knot rests on the other side of the karabiner, the role of the standing part and working end is reversed.

Form two loops and bring the two outer edges forward and together (step one). Make sure you have a Half Hitch and a turn (step two) before inserting the two bights into the karabiner. Apply load to the standing part, using the working end to provide control as the rope is paid out.

ITALIAN HITCH

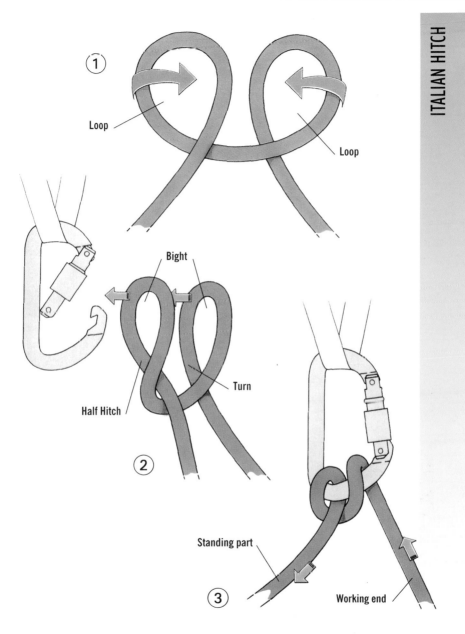

① Loop

Loop

② Bight

Turn

Half Hitch

③ Standing part

Working end

BARREL SLING

The Barrel Sling allows an open ended barrel or drum to be hoisted upright. Slide the rope under the barrel, bring both ends up and form an Overhand Knot (p.20). Splay the bights at each side of the barrel to make two Half Hitches. Join the ends of the strop with a Fisherman's Knot (p47). Before hoisting, take up the slack and adjust so that the barrel is central on the lower bight. Ensure that the bights around the girth are positioned above (but not too close to the top of) the centre of gravity of the barrel.

The Barrel Sling – the strop girth is positioned above the centre of gravity of the barrel

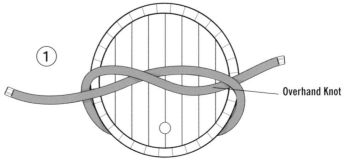

(1)

Overhand Knot

Half Hitch

Half Hitch

②

Fisherman's Knot

Strop

Join the ends of the strop between the hook and the barrel with a Fisherman's Knot (p. 47)

③

Lower bight

Never stand under a load being hoisted or lowered

TOP TIP

WAGGONER'S HITCH

Also known as: *Trucker's Hitch; Dolly*

For lashing down loads, the Waggoner's Hitch is unrivalled. Once mastered, its applications are numerous and it is easy to see why this knot is so popular. Apart from securing loads on waggons or trailers, it can be used as an emergency tackle (with care) and is ideal for use in guy lines that do not have adjusters.

Pull down on the working end to tighten the knot and secure with one or two Half Hitches (p.100). Like the Sheepshank (p.196) the Waggoner's Hitch is only secure when under constant strain.

TOP TIP

When using slippery rope, use a Slipped Overhand Loop (p.21) instead of a loop at the top of the hitch

The Waggoner's Hitch used to secure the lid of a chest

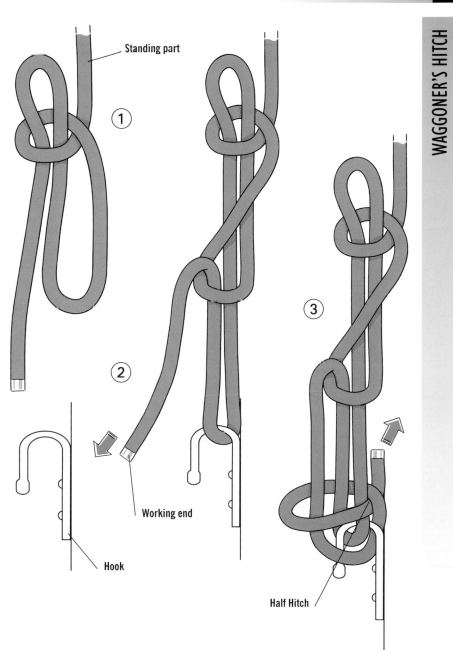

Standing part

(1)

(2)

(3)

Working end

Hook

Half Hitch

TUCKED HALF BLOOD KNOT

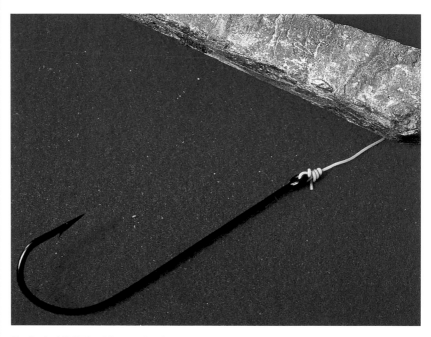

The Tucked Half Blood Knot used on hooks or swivels

The Tucked Half Blood Knot is used by anglers to attach a line to a hook eye or swivel. It is quick and easy to tie and holds well in monofilament line.

Before tying the knot, make the hook point and barb safe using a cork or similar material. To begin, pass the line through the eye of the hook. Make four turns of the working end around the standing part, then pass it back through the aperture between the eye and the turns to form a bight. Tuck the working end through the bight, and pull on the standing part to tighten the knot.

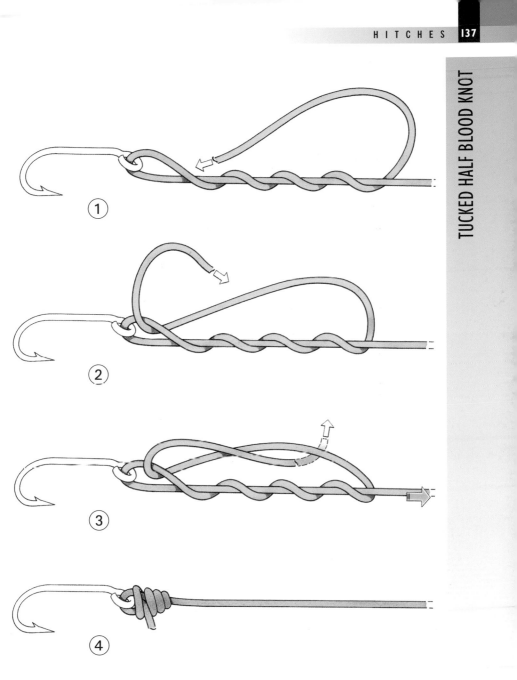

GRINNER KNOT
Also known as: *Uni-Knot*

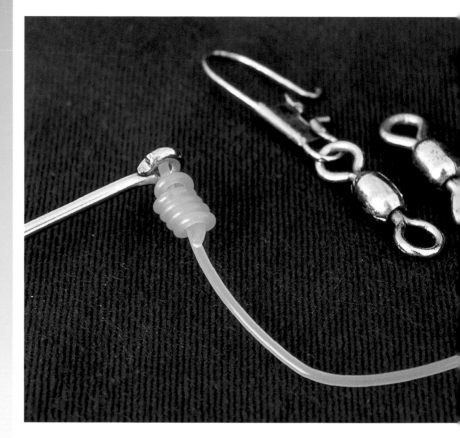

This tried and trusted knot is commonly used for joining lines to swivels, links or hooks. Make the point and barb of the hook safe in cork before you start; this will also increase your grip on the hook when pulling the knot up tight. Pass the line through the eye and double it back to form a loop (step one). Make four complete turns (step two), then pull on the standing part to tighten the knot. Remove any excess line from the working end, 3-5mm (⅛-¼in) from the knot.

The Grinner Knot, for attaching lines to hooks, links or swivels

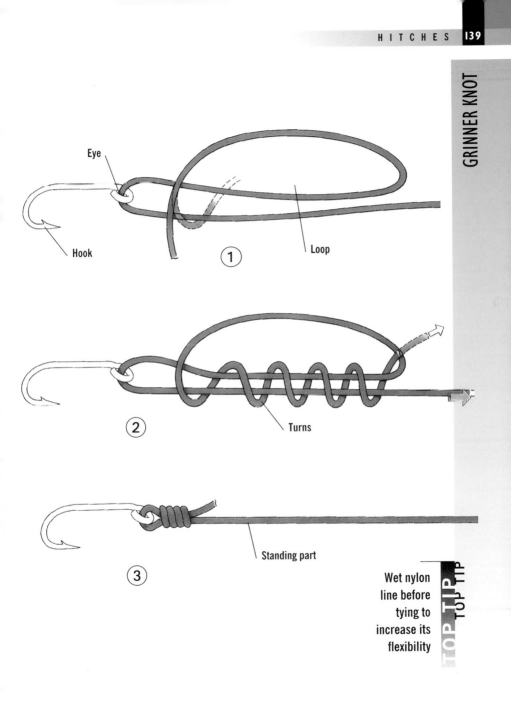

Eye

Hook

Loop

(1)

Turns

(2)

Standing part

(3)

TOP TIP

Wet nylon line before tying to increase its flexibility

TURLE KNOT

Simple to tie, the Turle Knot is used to tie hooks with angled eyes or "dry flies" to a tippet. Slip the line through the eye and position the hook away from the working end of the line (step one). Form an Overhand Noose (step two) and pass the hook through the loop (step three). Draw the knot up tight to provide a secure and neat attachment.

The Turle Knot, named after its founder, Major Turle

TOP TIP
Use this knot for attaching dry flies to a leader

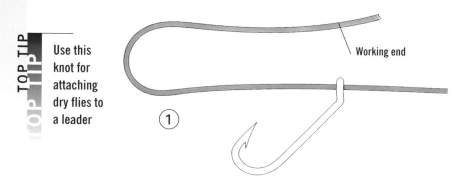

Working end

(1)

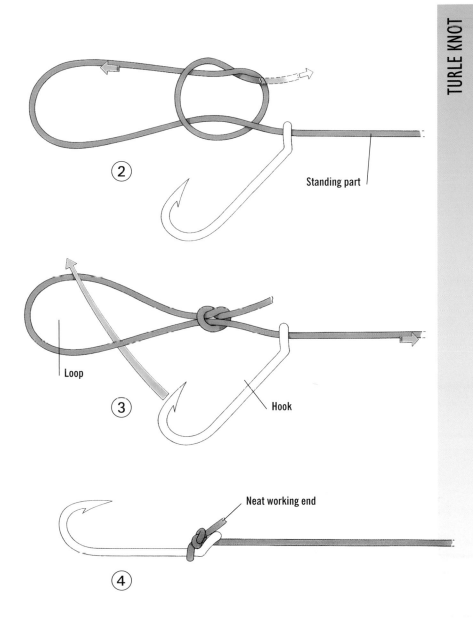

② Standing part

Loop

③ Hook

Neat working end

④

LOOP KNOTS

Loop knots are used to form either fixed or running, single, double or multiple loops in the end of a line or in a bight.

Uses for loop knots include:

A quick loop in the end or bight of light line –
Overhand Loop (p.144)

A loop in the end of a line (especially man-made fibre) –
Double Overhand Loop (p.145)
Angler's Loop (p.150)

A snare; a noose that will pull up tight and hold –
Poacher's Noose (p.146)

A secure, fixed loop for attaching the end or bight of a line –
Figure-of-Eight Loop (p.152)

A fixed loop through a ring –
Figure-of-Eight Loop (Threaded) (p.154)
Swami Loop (p.155)

A secure loop in the end of a line –
Bowline (p.156)

A fixed loop in rope that may become waterlogged –
Water Bowline (p.158)

To secure a line, which is under load, with a fixed loop –
Bowline, rope under tension (p.162)

To make a free running loop –
Running Bowline (p.166)

To make twin loops that can be adjusted for size –
Portuguese Bowline (p.170)

To make a fixed-loop foothold or handhold; to secure a bight in a line to a karabiner –
Alpine Butterfly Knot (p.172)

To make a loop in a paternoster to attach droppers –
Blood Loop Dropper Knot (p.174)

Form a fixed loop in a knife or whistle lanyard -
Lanyard Loop Knot (p.176)

To make a lariat or lasso, or a fixed loop in the end of a longbow string –
Honda Knot (p.178)

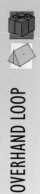

OVERHAND LOOP

The Overhand Loop is an extremely useful, quick and easy way of forming a loop in the end of a line. It can also be used to form a hitch on a ring by tying an Overhand Knot (p.20) and passing the working end through the ring to form a loop. Follow the path of the Overhand Knot back through so that the working end lies parallel with the standing part.

The Overhand Loop is not stable in synthetic lines and is difficult to untie after it has been under load, especially in small or natural fibre line.

An Overhand Loop is quickly formed in a bight at the end of, or mid-way along, a line

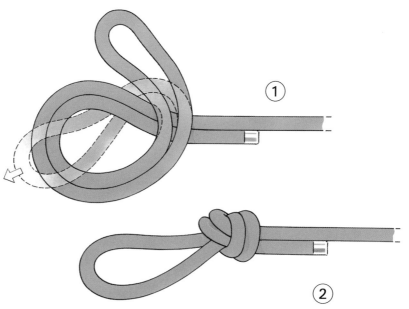

①

②

DOUBLE OVERHAND LOOP
Also known as: *Gut Knot*

This knot forms a secure fixed loop in the end of long-lines, leaders or snell, and has a number of other fixed-loop uses. It can be used in most materials, including fine wire, and also ties well in nylon fishing line. When using thicker and "springy" nylon lines, tie the knot around your index finger so that the line and first loop can be held by the thumb whilst tying.

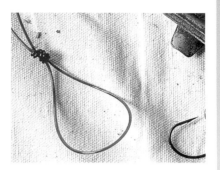

The Double Overhand Loop forms a secure loop in nylon fishing line

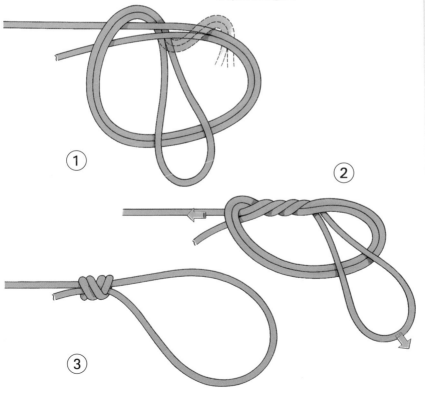

1

2

3

POACHER'S NOOSE
Also known as: *Double Overhand Noose*

This versatile and useful loop knot is well worth learning. In reality a Double Overhand Noose, the Poacher's Noose can be tied in almost any material from monofilament to small rope (including bungee cord). It forms a handsome noose, the slipping properties of which are adjusted by the tightness of the knot.

Another feature of the Poacher's Noose is that it holds well in most materials when tightened under load, which is why it makes a good snare for poachers. By inserting a nylon or metal thimble in the noose it can also be used to form a temporary hard eye.

Form a bight, then tie a Double Overhand Knot (p.22) using the grapevine method (step one). Pull the knot up, adjusting it to give the required slip on the noose. Pull on the standing part to tighten the noose.

TOP TIP

Adding one or two more turns will increase the friction applied by the knot, and also make it a little more decorative

The Poacher's Noose or Double Overhand Noose, tied using the grapevine method

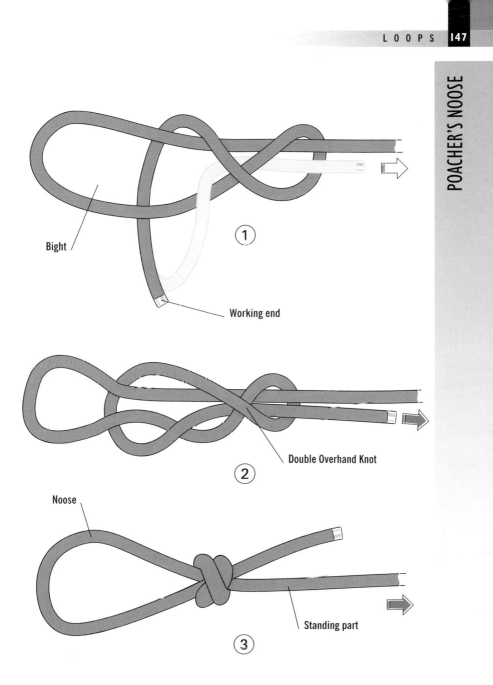

Bight

Working end

①

Double Overhand Knot

②

Noose

Standing part

③

ENGLISHMAN'S LOOP
Also known as: *Fisherman's Loop*

This loop dates back to the days when gut was used for fishing and, apart from the slippery nylons, it also holds well in most modern materials. To form this knot, tie a Slipped Overhand Knot (p.21) in the working end of a rope. Then form an Overhand Knot (p.20) in the working end around the standing part to act as a stopper and to determine the maximum size of the loop. Pull on the loop to slide the knots together and complete the Englishman's Loop.

An Englishman's Loop can be used to tie an adjustable loop in most materials

TOP TIP

Leave long ends on a stopper knot used in this way to prevent it from inadvertently coming undone

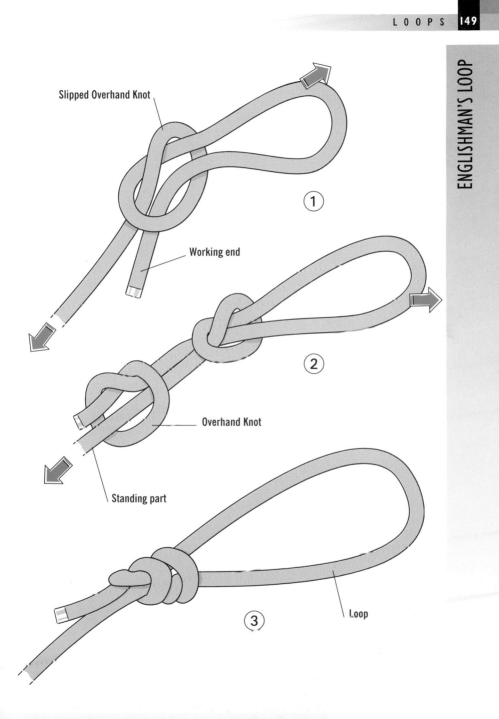

Slipped Overhand Knot

Working end

(1)

Overhand Knot

Standing part

(2)

Loop

(3)

ANGLER'S LOOP

The Angler's Loop is a handy, all-purpose, fixed loop that is stable when tied in cord or line. It is very quickly learned and tied, as it is derived from the Slipped Overhand Knot (p.21). Once placed under load this knot is difficult to untie, so unless you are forming a permanent loop or are prepared to cut the line, consider whether this is the best knot for the job.

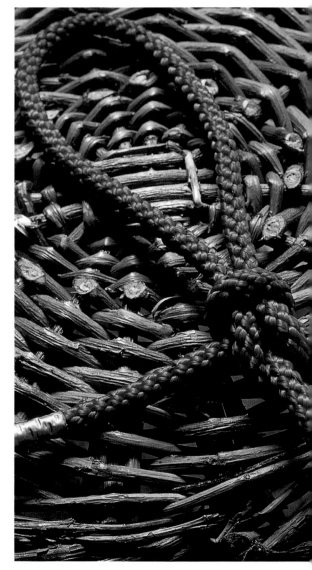

Make loops in the end of bungee (shock) cord with this knot. Ensure the knot is pulled up tight before use

The Angler's Loop is a quick and easy knot to tie

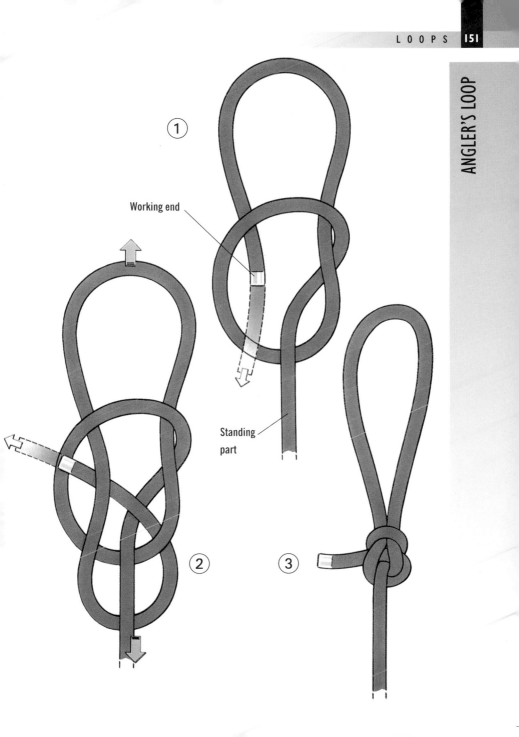

①

Working end

②

Standing
part

③

FIGURE-OF-EIGHT LOOP

Also known as: *Double Figure of Eight*

The Figure-of-Eight Loop is an easy knot to remember and tie

A Figure-of-Eight Loop can be tied in the bight of a rope if the two ends are not accessible, or in the end of a rope which has been doubled to make a bight. Either way, it makes a reliable fixed loop, which is easy to remember and tie. Its popularity with climbers, in preference to the Bowline (p.156), is due to the fact that it is easier to confirm that the Figure-of-Eight Loop is tied correctly.

When tying, pass the bight around the standing part(s) – do not be tempted to twist it into shape – then pull the knot up so that the leads lay neatly and parallel alongside each other. This knot can also be tied using the "Threaded" method (p.154).

FIGURE-OF-EIGHT LOOP

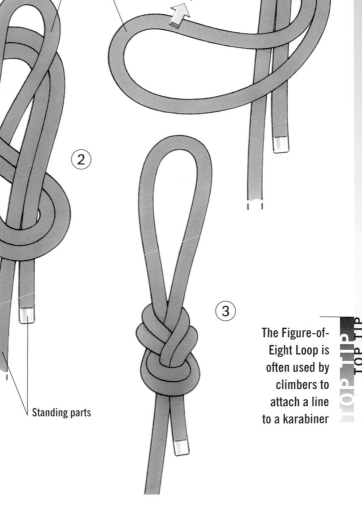

①

②

③

Bight

Standing parts

The Figure-of-Eight Loop is often used by climbers to attach a line to a karabiner

TOP TIP

FIGURE-OF-EIGHT LOOP (THREADED)

The Figure-of-Eight Loop tied through a ring

Use this method if the Figure-of-Eight Loop must be secured to a ring or other aperture. Tie a Figure-of-Eight Knot (p.26) in the standing part of the rope, pass the working end through the ring or aperture and work it back through the knot until the working end lays alongside the standing part. A Half Hitch (p.100) can be tied around the standing part to make the knot more secure.

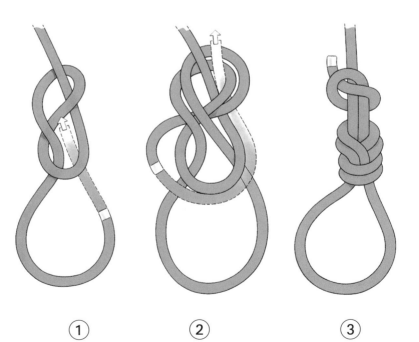

① ② ③

SWAMI LOOP

Also known as: *One-and-a-half Fisherman's Loop*

A Swami Loop with the Double Overhand Knot snug against the Slipped Overhand Knot

From monofilament to climbing ropes, this loop is useful to fishermen and climbers alike. It is easy to tie, secure and can also be used as a running loop. The maximum size of the loop is determined by the Double Overhand Knot (p.22), which sits snugly against the Slipped Overhand Knot (p.21). The Swami Loop can be used instead of the Figure-of-Eight Knot (p.26) to tie on to a climbing harness.

SWAMI LOOP

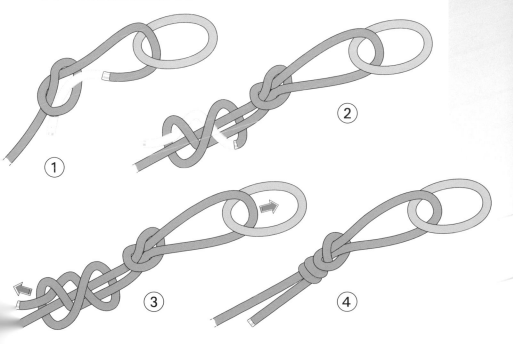

① ② ③ ④

BOWLINE

Knots with "bowline" in their name are numerous enough to have a treatise all to themselves. Only a small number of these, and various ways to tie them, have been included in this book. The Bowline is the most commonly used, generally for forming a fixed loop in the end of a line. Tried and tested over centuries, this knot is reliable, strong and stable, and can be tied using a variety of methods, making it suitable for all walks of life. Said to retain about 60 per cent of the strength of the line in which it is tied, the Common Bowline can be used for a variety of tasks. These include forming a temporary eye in a mooring rope, securing a line to a harness or ring, as a handhold at the end of a line and, in knots such as the Oklahoma Hitch (p.80), to unite the working end of a line with the standing part.

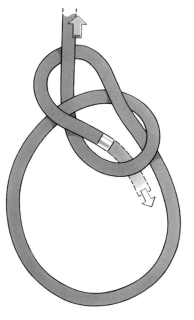

① ②

TOP TIP

To untie the Bowline when jammed, pull the bight around the standing part, forward and down towards the loop

The Bowline is a simple, strong and stable knot

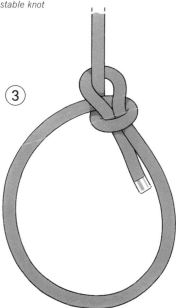

③

If the Bowline is tied too loosely it may turn into a slip knot. Always finish with a stopper knot for added security (above)

WATER BOWLINE

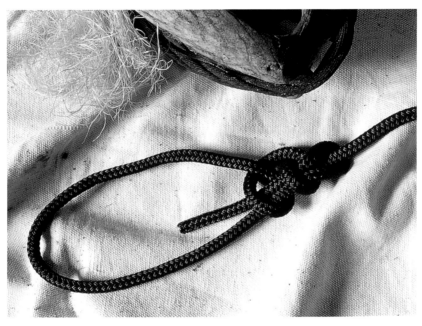

The Water Bowline – a trusty knot that can be untied even after it has been under strain in wet conditions

TOP TIP

Use this knot to secure a temporary line to a buoy and sinker

The extra turn in the standing part of this Bowline gives additional grip to the working end when under load. This results in a slightly more secure knot that will withstand rougher handling. Also, the bight around the standing part does not pull up so tightly because the load is supported more by the lower turn. Therefore, especially when wet, the Water Bowline is easier to untie than the Common Bowline (p.156).

Form two turns in the standing part. Pass the working end up through both turns, behind the standing part and down through both turns. Adjust the loop to the required size. Tighten the knot by pulling on the standing part and the loop.

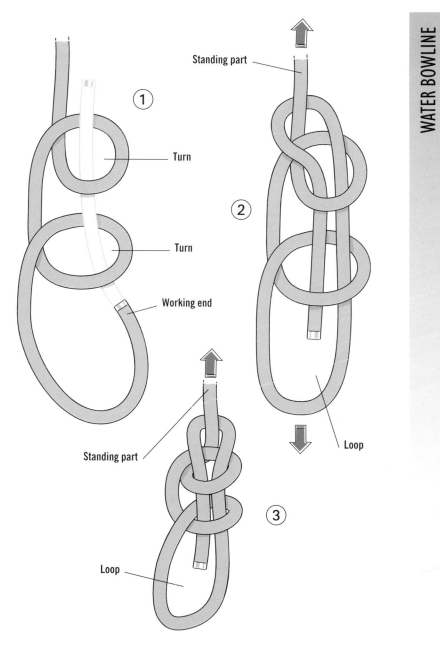

①

Turn

Turn

Working end

②

Standing part

Standing part

Loop

③

Loop

BOWLINE (CLIMBER'S)

Also known as: *Bulin Knot*

The Bowline with a Half Hitch in the working end for added security

This method of tying a Bowline was developed by climbers and is identical to the Bowline (p.156) when pulled up. When learning to tie the Bowline using this method you will, no doubt, discover that it is an Overhand Noose with the working end of the loop passed through the noose, which is then capsized by pulling on the standing part to form the Bowline.

Having mastered this tying method, try passing the working end around an object before tying the knot, but, before capsizing it, pull on the working end to take the knot close up to the object. Take time to perfect this technique, and learn the advantages of using this method – it can be quite rewarding.

(1)

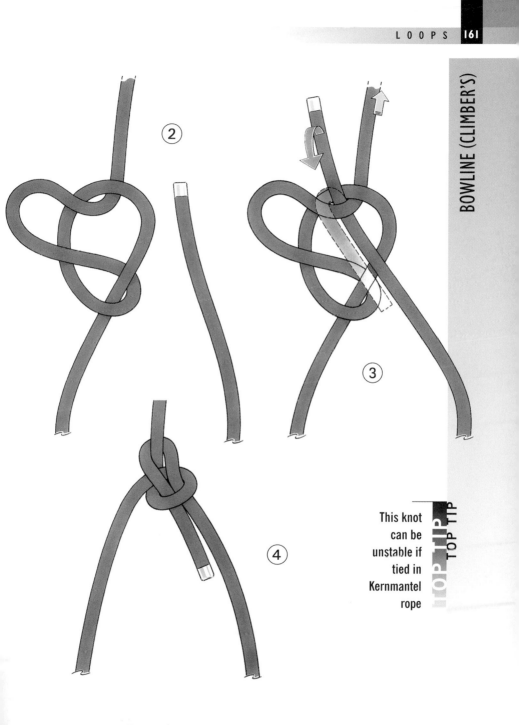

② ③ ④

TOP TIP

This knot can be unstable if tied in Kernmantel rope

BOWLINE, ROPE UNDER TENSION

This method of tying the Bowline will only work if the rope is large enough to capsize the Overhand Knot (p.20) into a loop, especially if the load is constant. Few people learn to tie a Bowline towards them and, when the occasion arises, they tend to become involuntary contortionists. Practice using this method to save any such embarrassment and enhance your knotting skills.

This Bowline, although tied with the rope under tension, is identical to the Common Bowline

BOWLINE, ROPE UNDER TENSION

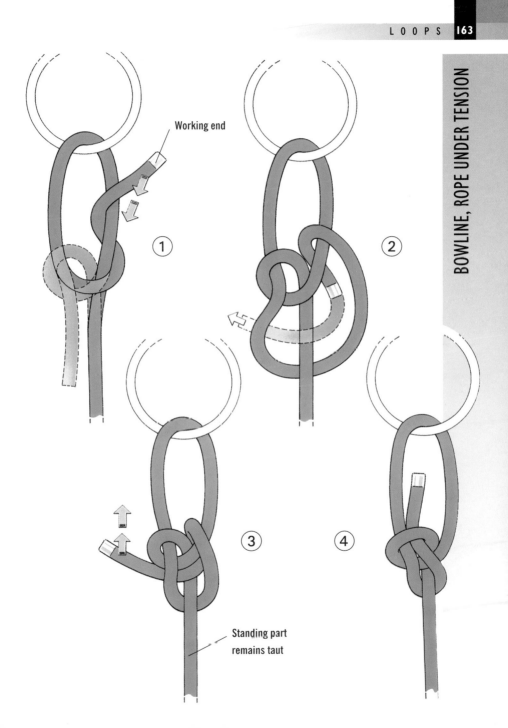

Working end

1

2

3

4

Standing part
remains taut

BOWLINE ON A BIGHT

This method is used to tie a loop in the middle of a rope when the ends are inaccessible, or to provide two loops in the end of a line. Because the two loops are in fact one loop doubled, each can be adjusted for size before pulling the knot up. This knot can be used as a sling or to seat an able person in an emergency rescue situation. It can also be used as a bosun's chair – the double loops being more comfortable than a single loop. The weight can be supported on either one or both of the standing parts.

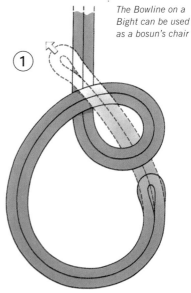

The Bowline on a Bight can be used as a bosun's chair

(1)

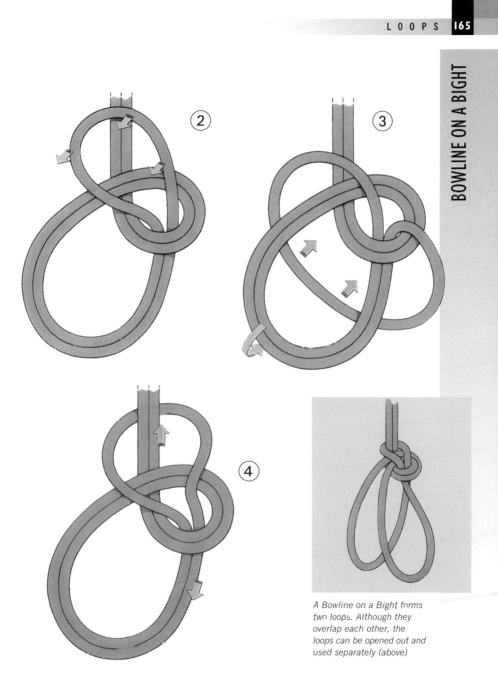

A Bowline on a Bight forms two loops. Although they overlap each other, the loops can be opened out and used separately (above)

RUNNING BOWLINE

The Running Bowline makes a simple running loop

The Running Bowline is probably the most popular of the running loops. It consists of the loop of a Bowline tied around its own standing part and can be tied in all forms of material. It can be used for such diverse purposes as making snares or to hoist an inanimate soft load like a sack of grain. With a light control line attached to the working end of the bowline, the noose can also be lowered into a crevasse or into water to recover lost objects. The weight of the object, combined with the pull on the standing part, creates the tension needed to make the knot grip. This means that the knot is only secure when under constant load.

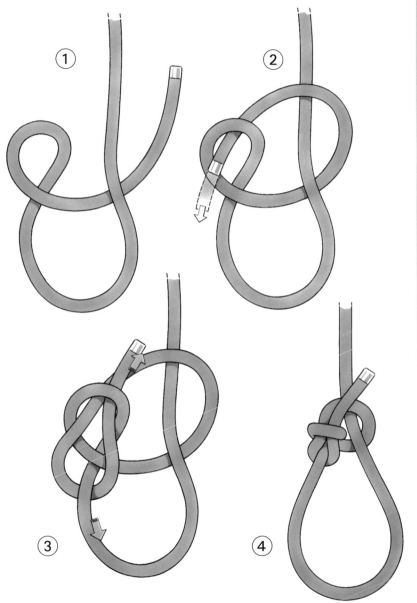

SPANISH BOWLINE

Like the Bowline on a Bight (p.164), the Spanish Bowline provides two loops in the middle of a rope or on a bight at the end. The two loops are independent and hold securely when under strain but, because they are connected through the centre of the knot, they can be adjusted for size before a load is applied. This is a useful knot for slinging and light rescue.

The Spanish Bowline provides two loops – useful for slinging and light rescue

①

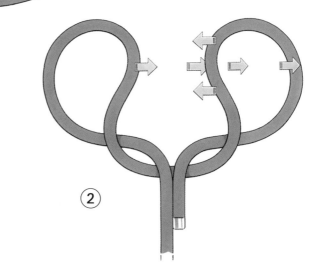

②

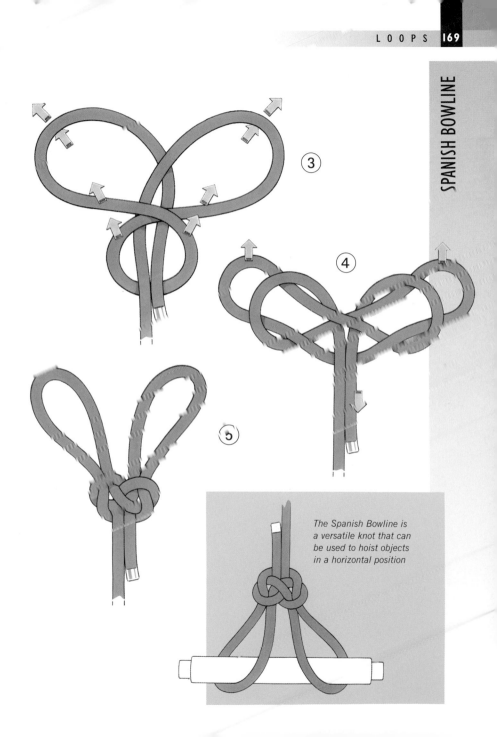

③

④

⑤

The Spanish Bowline is a versatile knot that can be used to hoist objects in a horizontal position

PORTUGUESE BOWLINE

The Portuguese Bowline provides two easily adjustable loops

This knot will be useful if the loops need to be balanced or adjusted to suit a particular load. Remember that the two loops are really just one loop doubled, and therefore an uneven load may cause one loop to extend and the other to contract. Adjust the loops to suit the task before tightening the knot. A four-loop knot can be formed by tying it on the bight. Using the bight as a working end, proceed as shown (opposite), but pass the bight the same way as you would for Bowline on a Bight (p.165).

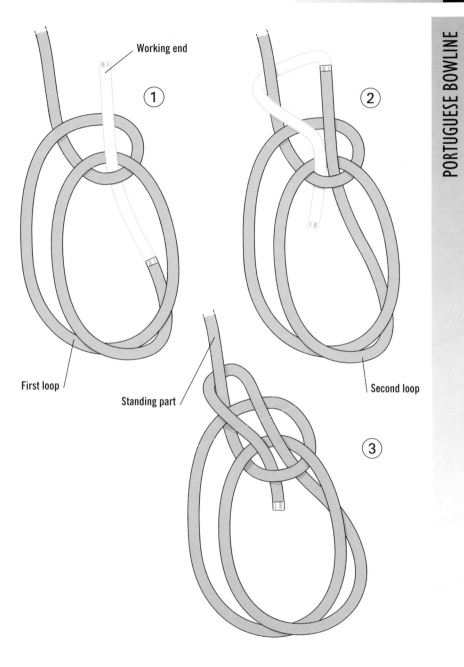

Working end

First loop

Standing part

Second loop

ALPINE BUTTERFLY KNOT

This elegant, versatile single loop can be tied in the middle of a rope with or without having access to the ends. Its main advantage over other loops is that it will take a load in any of three directions, independently or together. Depicted here is just one of the many different ways of tying this knot; if shown in other ways you should select the method most suited to you.

The many uses of the Alpine Butterfly Knot include: forming a temporary rope ladder (or étrier); securing the middle of a line to a karabiner; a temporary chest harness for light rescue; hoisting or lowering equipment where both ends of the line are attended to keep the load away from the face of a wall, cliff or obstruction.

The Alpine Butterfly will take a load in any of three directions, independently or together

①

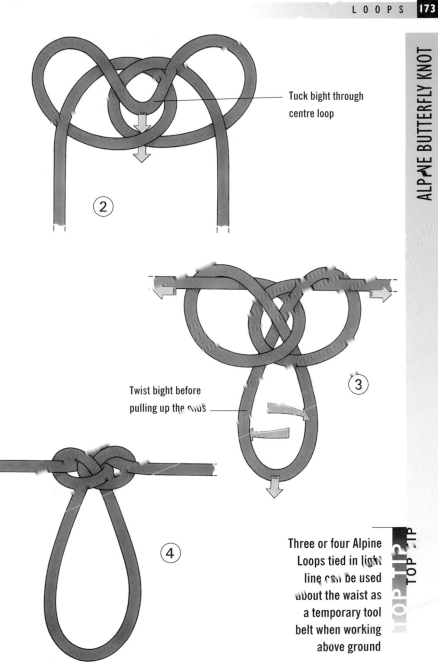

Tuck bight through
centre loop

②

Twist bight before
pulling up the ends

③

④

Three or four Alpine
Loops tied in light
line can be used
about the waist as
a temporary tool
belt when working
above ground

TOP TIP

BLOOD LOOP DROPPER KNOT

Also known as: *Dropper Loop*

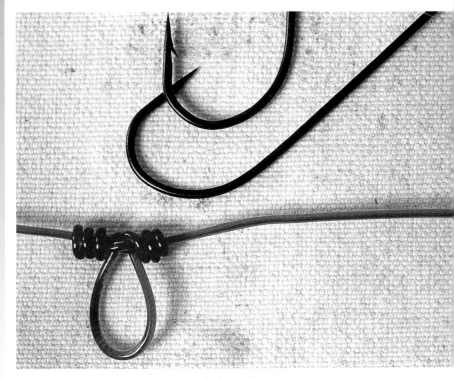

The Blood Loop Dropper Knot is also known as the Dropper Loop

This loop is made in a paternoster, the weighted line that carries a series of hooks along its length. Each hook line is known as a "dropper", hence the name given to this knot. Normally used in nylon line, it forms a convenient loop at right angles to the paternoster to which droppers can be attached. The Blood Loop Dropper Knot can be used in other types of line to provide convenient loops from which to hang items.

Begin the knot by forming an Overhand Knot (p.20) with a large loop. Make four or more tucks with each end before tucking the bight of the loop through the centre and pulling up the knot.

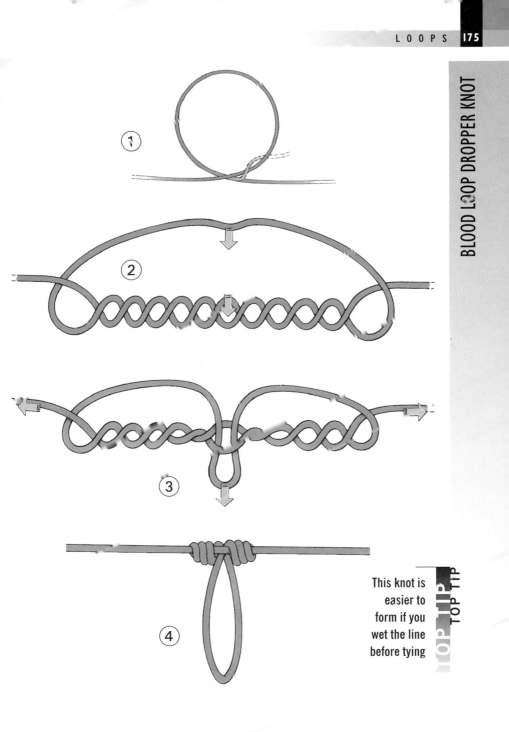

This knot is easier to form if you wet the line before tying

TOP TIP

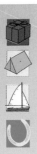

LANYARD LOOP KNOT
Also known as: *Single Strand Diamond Knot*

The Lanyard Loop Knot makes an attractive loop on the end of a knife or whistle lanyard

TOP TIP
Form an attractive button knot by pulling the loop into the knot and securing it with a stitch

There are several ways in which this attractive loop can be used. In neck or waist lanyards it forms a permanent loop for attaching items using a Ring Hitch (p.104), or the working end can be passed through a ring or D-handle to form the loop before the knot is tied. The Lanyard Loop can also be used as a necklace and the two hanging ends decorated with Multiple Overhand Knots (p.22). The ends of the rope or cord can then be teased out into a tassel.

Form a Carrick Bend (p.52) in the bight of the cord, with ends A and B emerging on opposite sides of the knot (step one). Pass end A over the loop, underneath and up through the centre of the knot (step two). Repeat for end B. Pull up gently and work the knot into shape.

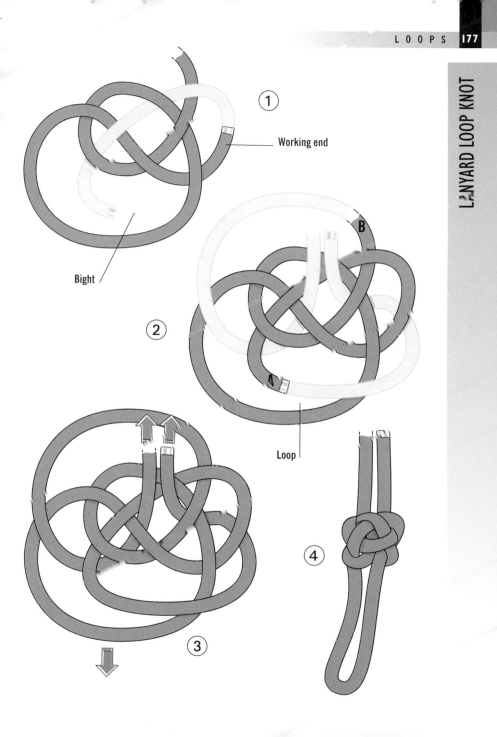

① Working end

Bight

② B

Loop

③

④

HONDA KNOT
Also known as: *Bowstring Knot*

Unlike the Slipped Overhand Knot (p.21) which forms an oval loop, the Honda Knot provides a round loop in the end of a line. It is also favoured to make a lariat (commonly known as a lasso or sliding loop) and, because the loop size can be adjusted with the overhand stopper knot, the Honda Knot is also suitable for use in the end of a longbow string.

To alter the size of the loop, pull it up to the required size, mark the line, then move the overhand knot up to the mark. To make a lariat, pull a bight through the fixed loop (step three). This running line will draw up instantly.

The Honda Knot forms a round loop in the end of a rope or line

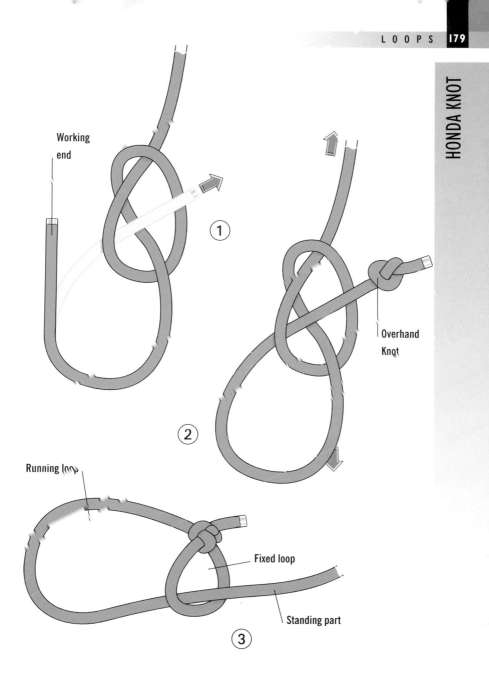

Working
end

1

Overhand
Knot

2

Running loop

Fixed loop

Standing part

3

HANDCUFF KNOT

A Handcuff Knot
before being
secured

TOP TIP

**Tie-back ends
can be
decorated with
a Multiple
Overhand Knot
and the ends
teased out to
form a tassel**

Apart from its obvious use – to restrain the limbs of a person –
the Handcuff Knot can be used as a hobble (to restrict the
movement of an animal) by adjusting the loops to the required
size and securing the working ends with an Overhand Knot
(p.20) or a Reef Knot (p.72). The Handcuff Knot can also be
used as a decorative "tie back" to one or two hooks on the wall,
and forms the foundation for the Fireman's Chair Knot (p.182).

Form two loops, as if making a Clove Hitch (p.108), then
pass the left bight through the right from back to front, and
the right bight through the left from front to back (step one).
Pull the two loops to tighten the knot, and pull the working
end to adjust the size of the loops (step two). Finish with an
Overhand Knot or a Reef Knot (step three).

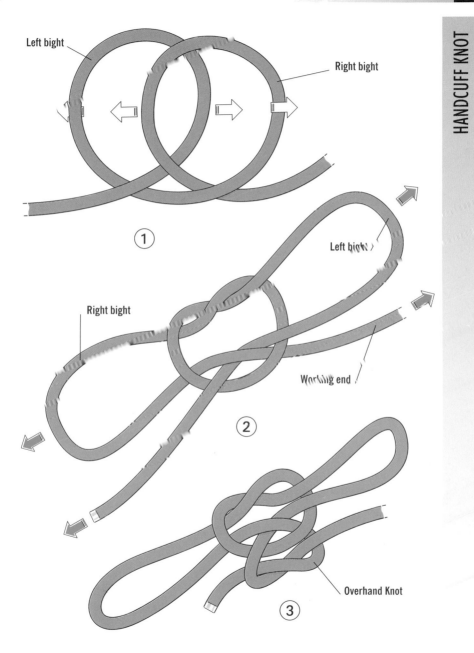

Left bight

Right bight

(1)

Left bight

Right bight

Working end

(2)

Overhand Knot

(3)

FIREMAN'S CHAIR KNOT

A Fireman's Chair Knot, tied in the bight of a light rescue line

In the event that a proper harness is not available, the
Fireman's Chair Knot can be used for light rescue. Start with
a Handcuff Knot (p.180) tied in the bight near the centre of
the rope. Adjust the loops to the required size to support the
legs (under the knees) and torso (under the arms). Tie off
with a Half Hitch (p.100) around each loop, then pull up
both Half Hitches tight against the centre knot. Use one end
to lower the person and the other (from below) to steady and
keep them away from obstructions.

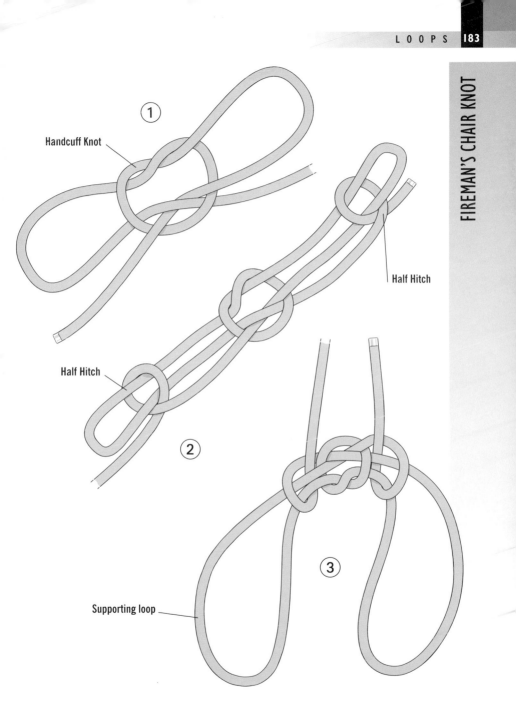

① Handcuff Knot

Half Hitch

Half Hitch

②

③

Supporting loop

HACKAMORE KNOT

Also known as: *Bottle or Jug Sling (when tied in single line)*

Originally part of the Hackamore or emergency bridle, this knot seems to be disappearing from general use in horse tack. However, it is a handsome knot that should be preserved as it has many practical uses and can also be used for decorative work.

To use this knot as a bottle or jug sling, tie in single, rather than double, line. Insert the neck of the bottle in the centre of the knot, pull up tight and tie the two ends through the loop to form a handle.

Closely associated with the Hackamore Knot is the Fiadore Knot (p.202).

You will need approximately 2m (6ft) of rope or line to tie this knot

The Hackamore Knot, a handsome as well as practical knot

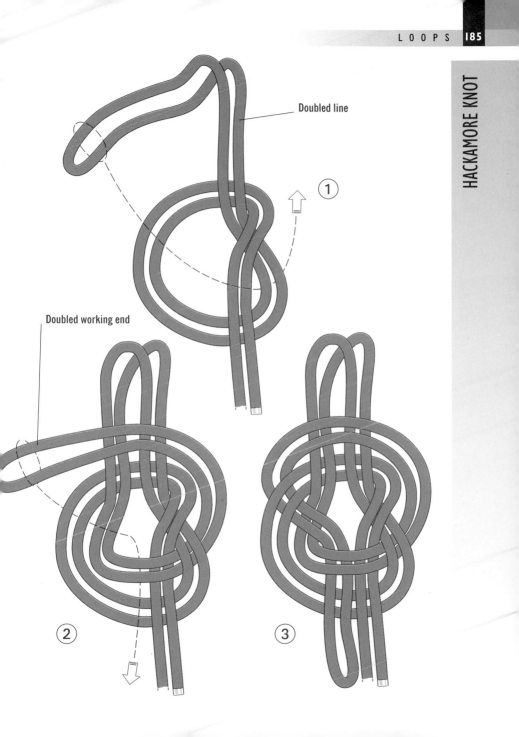

Doubled line

①

Doubled working end

②

③

MISCELLANEOUS AND DECORATIVE KNOTS

This section features those knots that do not fit neatly into the previous categories. These can be used to shorten and splice rope, make temporary fixings, embellish clothing and hardware and to make useful or decorative articles with which to adorn your home, boat, den, shack or garden.

Uses for miscellaneous and decorative knots include:

To shorten a rope or make a single strand decorative braid –
Chain Sennit (p.188)

To make a permanent fixed eye in the end of a rope –
Eye Splice (p.190)

To make a join in identical stranded rope –
Short Splice (p.192)

To prevent the end of a rope from unravelling –
Back Splice (p.194)

To temporarily shorten or take strain from the damaged part of a rope –
Sheepshank (p.196)

To make a rope ring or bracelet –
Grommet (p.197)

To make a guy or stay attachment for a temporary mast –
Jury Mast Knot (p.200)

To make a temporary rope ladder –
Rope Ladder Knot (p.204)

To make a rope tensioning device –
Poldo Tackle (p.206)

To make a decorative rope –
Round Crown Sennit (p.208)

To make a square braid –
Square Crown Sennit (p210)

To make a coaster or mat –
Ocean Plait Mat (p.212)

To cover a ring, rail or post with continuous hitching –
Cockscombing (p.214)

CHAIN SENNIT

Also known as: *Chain Shortening; Drummer's Plait; Bugler's Braid*

The Chain Sennit is both practical and decorative, as its many names suggest. For shortening a rope without cutting it, the chain sennit makes a secure knot which can easily be untied. As a decorative knot, it is often seen as part of the drag ropes on a military side drum, where its length can be adjusted to suit the height of the drummer.

Commence the Chain Sennit with a Slipped Overhand Knot (p.21). Pass a bight through the loop (step one) and pull the Overhand Knot up tight. Continue passing a bight through the previous loop and tightening the previous knot (step two). For a neat finish, make sure that the loops always lay in the same direction. Finish by passing the working end through the last loop.

TOP TIP

Use this knot to stow lines or ropes that will not coil easily or that need to be run out, in a hurry, without tangling. Quadruple the line and form the sennit loosely starting at the end with two bights

The Chain Sennit, made up snugly to form a drum drag rope

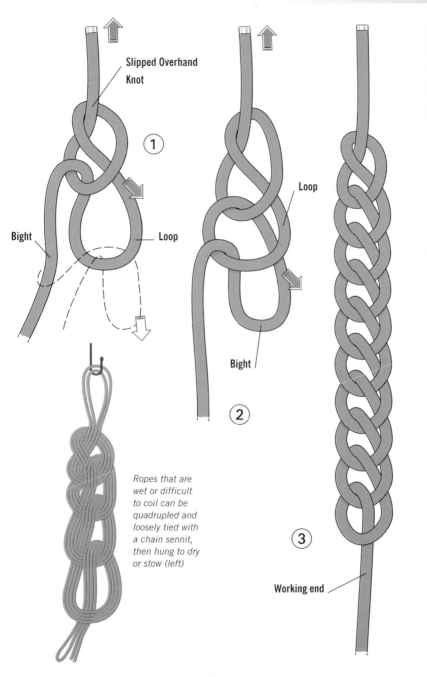

Slipped Overhand Knot

①

Bight

Loop

Loop

②

Bight

③

Working end

Ropes that are wet or difficult to coil can be quadrupled and loosely tied with a chain sennit, then hung to dry or stow (left)

EYE SPLICE

A soft Eye Splice in a tow-rope

This Eye Splice can only be formed using stranded rope; three or four strands are the most common. The splice forms an eye which can be left soft, or have a metal or nylon thimble inserted to form a hard eye.

Tape or stop the rope about 20cm (8in) from the working end, unlay the strands up to the stop and tape the ends to make them easier to tuck. Form a loop at the size of the required eye, then, starting with the centre strand, tuck it under one strand of the standing part (step one). Next, take the left strand and tuck it under the standing part strand to the left of the centre strand (step two). Turn the work over and tuck the remaining strand under the unoccupied strand in the standing part (step three). Continue tucking each strand over-under-over for the required number of tucks.

The advantage of using a splice rather than a loop knot is that the splice makes a permanent and neater eye, and the rope retains most, if not all, of its strength.

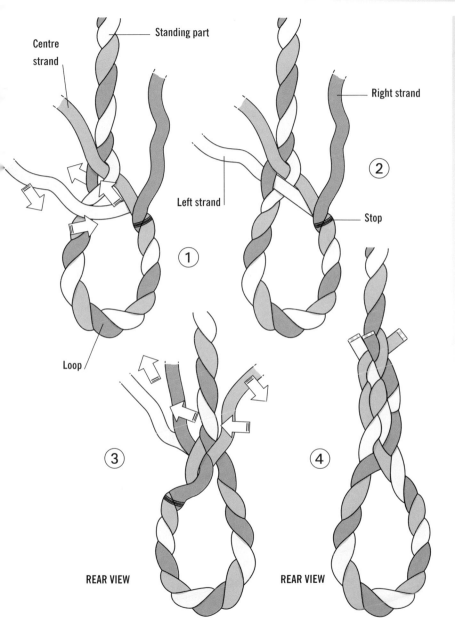

Standing part

Centre strand

Right strand

Left strand

Stop

①

②

Loop

③ REAR VIEW

④ REAR VIEW

SHORT SPLICE

The Short Splice can be used in three- or four-strand rope to join two identical ropes where the added diameter is of no consequence. Unlike bends, splicing retains most of the strength of a rope.

Put a temporary stop about 30cm (12in) from each end of the rope to be spliced. Unlay the strands and intertwine the ends (step one). Tuck each strand end under, over and under the strands laid up in the opposite rope. Repeat on both sides for at least three tucks, then finish by whipping or heat sealing the ends.

TOP TIP

Use at least three tucks, each side of the centre. Whip or hot-melt and tape the ends

A Short Splice repair in a broken rope

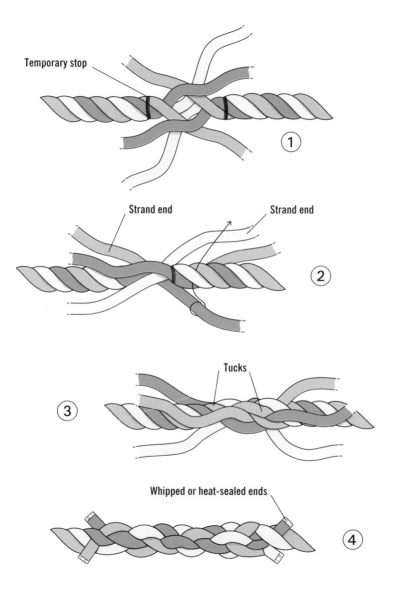

Temporary stop

Strand end   Strand end

①

②

Tucks

③

④

Whipped or heat-sealed ends

BACK SPLICE

The Back Splice stops the end of a rope from unlaying

The Back Splice is used to stop the end of a stranded rope from unlaying, especially when it is in constant use. A temporary whipping, or stop, is put around the rope at the point where the splice is to start (step one). The rope is then unlaid and a Crown Knot (p.33) formed above the temporary stop before the unlaid ends are spliced back into the standing part of the rope. Use at least three tucks, then taper down to the diameter of the rope by removing about one third of each strand. Make another two tucks, then, if necessary, hot-melt the ends or dog-ear half of each remaining strand with half of the adjacent one.

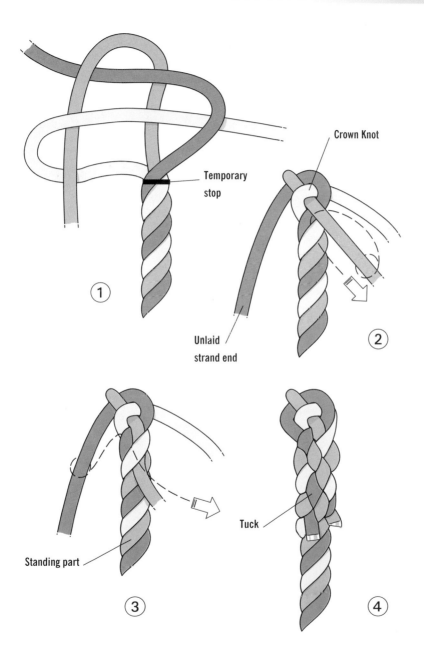

Temporary
stop

Crown Knot

Unlaid
strand end

① ②

Standing part

Tuck

③ ④

SHEEPSHANK

The sheepshank in its most basic form, shown here, is designed to shorten a length of line without it being cut. Another use is to render unused a damaged part of a line by positioning the damaged section in the centre loop. It is important to understand that the knot is only effective when under a constant load.

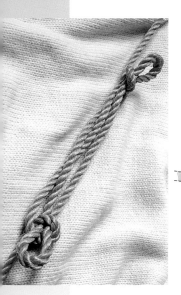

The Sheepshank
as a shortening

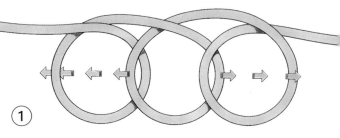

(1)

(2)

(3)

TOP TIP

If both rope ends are accessible, pass them through the loops to prevent the knot coming undone when it is not under load

ROPE GROMMET

A Grommet can be made with stranded rope or line, provided the strands will hold their shape when unlaid; unfortunately many man-made fibre ropes are laid up so loosely that once unlaid they will not readily lay back up. Commence the knot by cutting a length of rope at least three and a half times the circumference of the finished grommet. Tape the ends of each strand, then unlay one carefully so as to retain its shape. Form a loop with the strand (step one), laying a strand end in the grooves, following the loop all the way round. Now lay the other strand end around the loop

A neatly laid up Grommet makes an ideal deck quoit

ROPE GROMMET(CONTINUED)

in the opposite direction. A slight twist will help the strand end sit snugly in the lay of the rope to produce a neat, round Grommet that resembles the original rope. Divide the two strand ends in half and tie an Overhand Knot (p.20) using half of each end (step four). Make sure this knot is as tight as possible so that it fits snugly in the lay (this is best done around a fid or post). Unlay the strands of the rope and tuck them as flat as possible over and under the strands of the Grommet, as if making a splice (p.190–195). Cut the strand ends back for a neat finish.

Traditionally, Grommets are used to form the ring of a sewn eyelet or rope block strops, but they also make attractive bracelets, quoits or deck hockey pucks.

①

②

TOP TIP

By stretching the Grommet over a tapered fid to a marked point before pulling up the Overhand Knot, a set of Grommets can be made identical in size

③

④

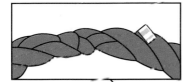

⑤

TOP TIP

For use as a quoit or hockey puck, cover the Grommet with coloured electrical insulation tape or heavy-duty duck tape

JURY MAST KNOT

The Jury Mast Knot – suitable for three or four guy lines

This knot makes an ideal point to secure three or four guy lines or stays to a temporary mast. The knot only provides attachment points for guy lines, it is not capable of gripping the mast. Therefore it should be secured to the mast above an existing fixing – such as a horizontal yard (or crosstree), a transom square lashed to the mast or in a groove cut into the mast – so that it will not slide down the mast when in use. Guy ropes or stays can be attached to the loops with a Sheet Bend (p.44). If a fourth stay or guy line is required, make another loop by tying the two working ends together with a Fisherman's Knot (p.47).

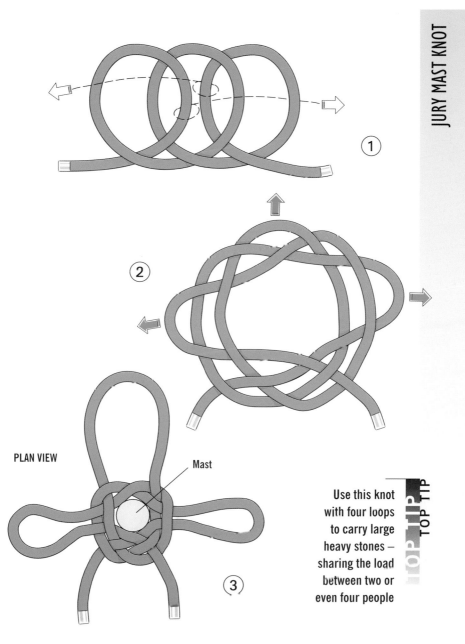

① ②

PLAN VIEW

Mast

③

FIADORE KNOT

Also known as: *Theodore Knot*

For many years this knot has been used with the Hackamore Knot (p.184), but so few people could tie it that it may well be the cause of the demise of what some consider to be the best headgear to rein in a horse. Here, thanks to Charlie Smith from Essex, is a method of tying this knot that even a novice can follow. Apart from its use alongside the Bosal and Hackamore Knot in a hackamore, the Fiadore Knot makes a handsome loop knot which can be used at camp, in the tool shed or even on a child's pushchair to suspend items using a Ring Hitch (p.104).

The Fiadore Knot – not as difficult as some would make out

①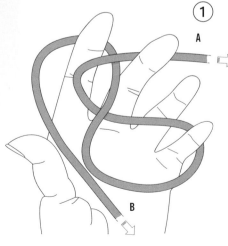

A

B

②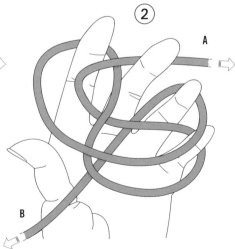

A

B

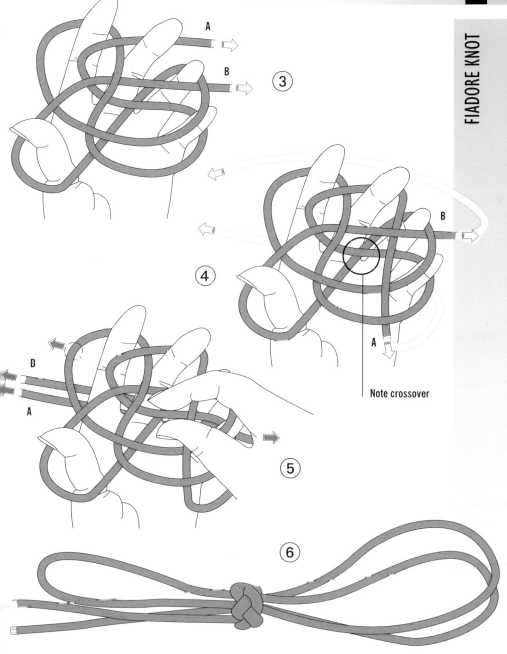

A

B

③

④

Note crossover

B

A

D

A

⑤

⑥

ROPE LADDER KNOT

The Rope Ladder Knot can be safely used to construct a temporary ladder; the rope can then be recovered for normal use afterwards. This knot also forms a ladder to suspend over the side of a boat, or from a tree house or play area. Use rope 12–25mm (½–1in) in diameter, and allow approximately 2m (6ft) of rope for each step. Rungs should be 12–15cm (5–6in) wide, and positioned 24–30cm (10–12in) apart.

TOP TIP

Flexible ladders such as this, when suspended without any rear support, are best climbed and descended facing one edge, with one hand and foot on each side

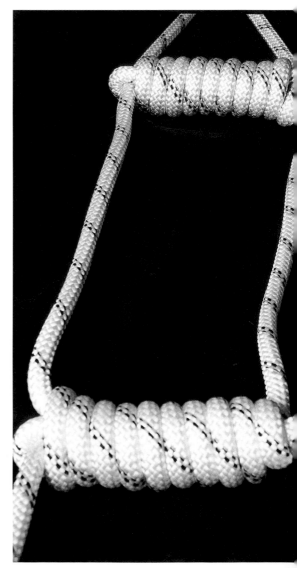

When suspended from the side of a boat, the Rope Ladder Knot is a useful climbing aid for swimmers

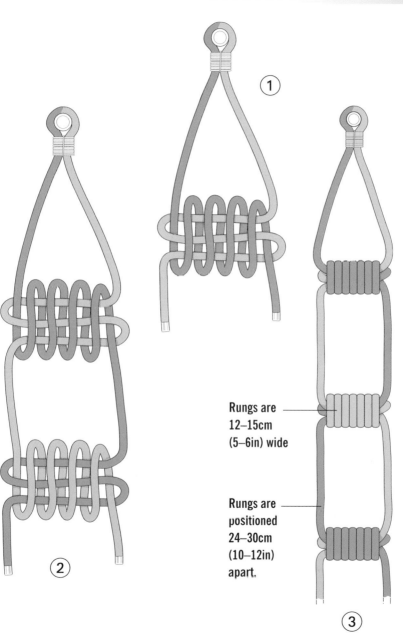

①

②

Rungs are
12–15cm
(5–6in) wide

Rungs are
positioned
24–30cm
(10–12in)
apart.

③

POLDO TACKLE

The Poldo Tackle provides an adjustable tensioning device

TOP TIP Remember that the two knots and the sharp bends in the line will reduce the breaking strain of the rope; do not overload it

Really another "jury rig" device, the Poldo Tackle is used to apply and release tension on whatever it is attached to – tensioning barriers or ridge ropes, aligning fence posts and tensioning anchor cables are but a few of its many uses. The Poldo Tackle can also be used to adjust the height of, or lift and lower, light loads over a small distance, for example the camp food safe, shower head or billy cans.

Tie a Bowline (p.146) with a small loop in one end of the line. Pass the standing part around a static point and back through the loop in the Bowline (step one). Pass the standing part around the second object, then form another Bowline with its loop around the standing part (step two). Pull the standing part to release tension, and pull either Bowline to tighten the tackle.

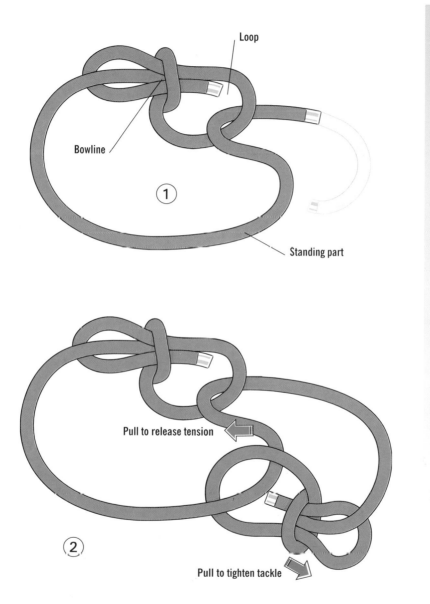

Loop

Bowline

① 1

Standing part

Pull to release tension

② 2

Pull to tighten tackle

ROUND CROWN SENNIT

Continuous crowning of three or more lines will form a decorative rope. In most materials, up to six cords will be self supporting; any more will need to be formed around a core. The secret of an attractive finish is ensuring that the tension on each cord is the same for every crown. To make a small lanyard for pocket or belt tools, (for ease of handling in cold or wet conditions), pass two cords through the tool ring until they are doubled, tie a stop or tape around all four at the length required, and crown the four ends back towards the tool using the cord below the stop as a core. Crown to the left (as shown) or to the right, but be sure to continue in one direction only. Finally, thread the ends back up into the crowning, out through the side and cut off any excess.

The Round Crown Sennit makes an attractive rope or tool lanyard

TOP TIP

To create an attractive spiral finish, try using different colour cords

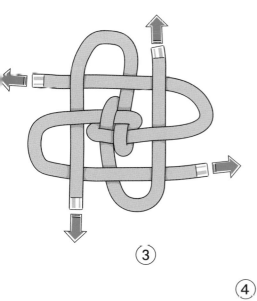

(1)

(2)

(3)

(4)

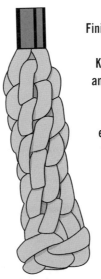

TOP TIP

Finish with tape or tie a Wall Knot and then another Crown Knot before pushing the ends through the centre of the sennit

SQUARE CROWN SENNIT
Also known as: *Nelson Sennit; Alternate Crown Sennit*

The Square Crown Sennit can be tied in four single cords, four pairs or – for the really adventurous – four triple cords.

Form the Sennit by first tying a left-hand Crown Knot (p.33), then a right-hand Crown Knot on top of it. Follow with alternate left- and right-hand Crowns, each pulled up as evenly as possible.

The finished knot makes a decorative lanyard, bag handle or bell rope.

TOP TIP

Try this knot using double cords for a bulkier finish. Different coloured cords also combine well in this knot

The Square Crown Sennit makes an attractive decorative plait

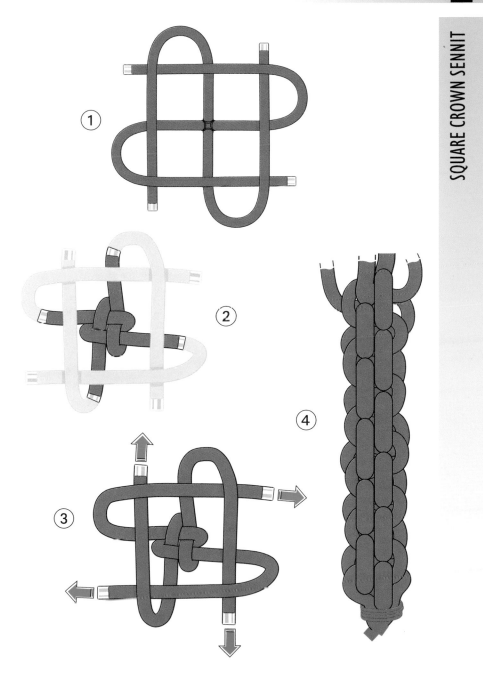

OCEAN PLAIT MAT

*An Ocean Plait
Mat for use as
a step tread*

Old or damaged rope can be put to good practical use by
making mats such as this one. Start by making a bight at just
over one-third the distance from one end of the rope and
form a loose knot (step one). When the foundation is
complete, the double or treble passes around the knot are
woven in both directions using the remaining rope. To finish,
whip the ends of the rope and sew them to the underside of
the mat with whipping twine or carpet thread.

One note of caution: the amount of cordage used in mats
such as this can be deceptive. For example, this mat (above)
measures 38 x 20cm (15 x 8in) and requires approximately
12m (40ft) of 10mm (¹/₂in) cordage.

COCKSCOMBING

Also known as: *Ringbolt Hitching*

Cockscombing – a practical, yet decorative protection

Originally used to protect lines that passed through ringbolts, this decorative form of hitching has become popular for decorating rings, rails, jug handles and such like. Three-strand Cockscomb (right) is the most common, but combinations using pairs and a greater number of cords are also used. If it is not possible to cover the strand ends, tape them to the object you are covering so that they will lie under the finished knot. When the Cockscombing is complete, thread the final ends under the knot and back out. Pull and cut the ends so that they then shrink back inside the knot.

TOP TIP

When covering a ring or an eye, form the ridge of the Cockscombing on the outer circumference

COCKSCOMBING

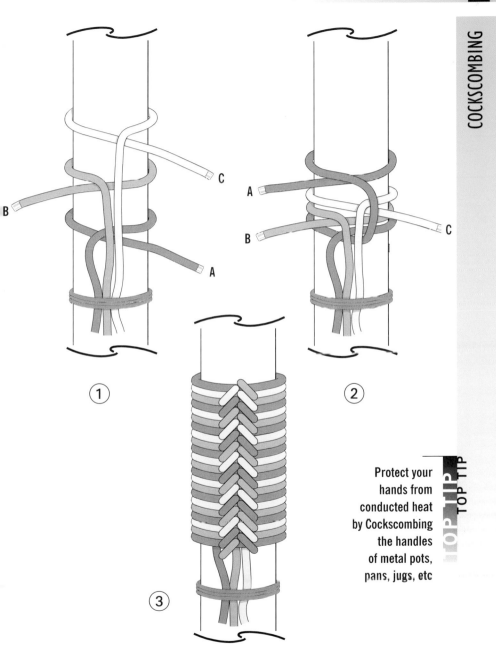

B

C

A

A

B

C

(1)

(2)

(3)

Protect your
hands from
conducted heat
by Cockscombing
the handles
of metal pots,
pans, jugs, etc

TOP TIP

GLOSSARY

Backing line – monofilament or braided polyester line with a breaking strain of 7–9kg (15–19lb), used under the fly-line to bulk out a fly-reel spool. It prevents the fine fly-line from twisting and forming into tight coils.

Bend – describes the action of tying two ropes together by their ends.

Bight – any part of a rope between the two ends, especially when slack and bent back on itself to form a loop (p.17). A knot tied "in the bight" or "on the bight" does not require the ends for the tying process.

Bosal – soft nose band for the hackamore. Usually braided using cords or leather.

Breaking Strain or **Breaking Strength (BS)** – the rope manufacturer's calculation of the average load that will cause an unused rope to break (*see* Safe Working Load, which can be as little as six per cent of the breaking strain).

Butt – the thick part of a leader, the other section having been joined to the fly-line. The butt is usually mono-filament with a breaking strain of 9–10kg (19-22lb), although braided line is sometimes used.

Cable – a large rope or anchor warp or chain.

Cable laid – rope formed of three right-handed hawsers laid up left-handed to form a larger nine-strand rope or cable.

Capsize – describes the change in the form of a knot. This can either be accidental – where stresses are applied to a loose or wrongly pulled-up knot causing the knot to become insecure, or deliberate – when forces are applied to parts of the knot to make it easier to untie. There are also knots that can be correctly tied by capsizing another knot form.

Clear – describes the action of loosening tangles in ropes.

Cleat – a wood or metal fitting with two horns, to which ropes are belayed. Typically used for securing flag and sail halyards or as a deck fitting for securing mooring lines or sheets.

Cord – the name given to several tightly twisted or plaited yarns, which make a line with a diameter of less than 10mm (½ in).

Cordage – the collective name for ropes and cords.

Core or **heart** – the inner part or heart of a rope or sinnet of more than three strands and in most braided lines. The core is formed from a loosely twisted strand, or from a bundle of parallel yarns or plaited strands, and runs the length of the rope. It may be just a filler or serve as the main strength-bearer in braided ropes.

Double line – similar to a loop, but both parts of the line are used together rather than working with the loop that is formed.

Dropper – a short length of monofilament bearing a wet fly and the fly-line. Some leaders are commercially made with droppers attached; alternatively, droppers may be attached to a plain leader with a Blood Knot (p.60).

End – usually the end of a length of rope that is being knotted (*see* standing part *and* working end).

Eye – a loop formed at the end of a length of rope by knotting, seizing or splicing (p.17). Also an aperture in a hook, thimble or needle through which a line can be threaded.

Fid – a tapering wooden pin used to work or loosen strands of a rope.

Foul – describes a rope that cannot slide because it is tangled or caught.

Frapping turns – those turns around a lashing which serve to tighten it before the end is secured.

Fray – describes the unravelling, especially of the end, of a length of rope.

Grommet – a ring of stranded rope, made up using one strand laid around itself three times.

Guy lines – stays of rope or wire, which serve to hold a mast, sheers, posts, tents and so on, in position.

Hackamore – a Western bridle without a bit, used to break in horses.

Hard laid – tightly laid-up rope, which can be stiff and difficult to knot or coil.

Hawser – a rope or cable large enough for towing or mooring.

Heart – *see* core.

Heaving line – a light line, typically 8mm ($^5/_{16}$in) in diameter and about 30m (98ft) long, with a Monkey's Fist (p.30) or a Heaving Line Knot (p.28) on the end as a weight. The line is coiled, then the weighted end thrown with an over-arm action. Used to haul a heavier rope, normally from ship to shore.

Hitch – a knot that secures a rope to a post, ring, spar, etc. or to another rope.

Hobble – rope or tape used to tether one or more of the feet of a domestic animal

Karabiner – a metal coupling link with a safety closure – used mainly for industrial roping, climbing and caving.

Kernmantel – method of rope construction consisting of a core of filaments over which a tight outer sheath of braided fibres is fitted.

Lanyard – a short rope or cord, usually three stranded and often braided or ornamented, used to secure objects or rigging, or as a safety line on tools and equipment when working above ground.

Lariat or **Lasso** – rope with a running noose, used to ensnare animals from horseback.

Lay – the direction of the twist of the strands forming a rope. Can be either left- or right-handed.

Lay up – the re-laying of the strands of a rope that have been unlaid, to restore the rope to its original form.

Lead – the direction taken by the working end through a knot.

Leader – the length of nylon that forms the junction between the fly-line and the fly.

Line – the generic name for cordage with no specific purpose, although it may also refer to rope with a definite use, such as fishing line or a clothesline.

Loop – part of a rope bent so that its parts come together (p.17).

Marline – a thin line of two (often loosely twisted) strands, traditionally left-hand laid. Used for seizing, marling, and so on.

Marling – the act of lashing or binding with marline, taking a hitch at each turn.

Marlinespike – a pointed iron instrument for separating the strands of a rope (especially wire) when splicing. Can also be used as a lever to tighten seizing.

Multi-plait – strong but flexible rope that does not kink, plaited using four or six pairs of strands, half of which are right-hand laid, and half left-hand laid.

Nip – the binding pressure within a knot that prevents it from slipping.

Noose – a loop formed by the working end being tied around the standing part of a rope in such a way that, when the standing part is pulled or the loop pulled away from the standing part, it draws up tight.

Reeve – describes the act of passing the end of a rope through a block, ring or cleat.

Rope – general term used for cordage

that has a diameter of more than 10mm (½in). Also used to specify a rope, such as bell rope, guy rope, bolt rope, etc.

Safe Working Load (SWL) – the estimated load that can be placed on a rope without it breaking, given its age, condition, the knots used and any shock loading. Note: safe working load may be as little as six per cent of the manufacturer's quoted breaking strength.

Seizing – binding with turns of small stuff, which secures two parts of the same rope together (p.17) or one rope parallel to another.

Sennit or **sinnet** – braided cordage made in flat, round or square form using three or more strands.

Slack – the part of a rope that is not under tension.

S-laid rope – left-hand laid rope.

Small stuff – twine, string, line or cord with a diameter of less than 10mm (½in).

Soft laid – loosely laid-up rope.

Splice – describes the act of joining the ends, or the end and a standing part, of rope by interweaving strands.

Standing part – the part of a rope that is fixed or under tension (p.17), as opposed to the end that is free (the working end) with which the knot is tied.

Stop – a binding knot or whipping used as a temporary measure to stop a rope from unravelling.

Stopper – a short length of rope or chain, secured at one end. Used to control the running out or to secure another rope.

Strand – yarns twisted together in the opposite direction to the yarn itself. Rope made with twisted strands (not braided) is known as laid line.

Strop or **Sling** – a continuous band of rope or webbing tape that is used as a support or lifting aid. Can be either manufactured for the purpose or made by joining two ends of a rope or tape with a suitable bend.

Tag end – the part of a fishing line in which the knot is tied (*see* working end).

Tippet or **Point** – the thin, terminal section of the leader to which a fly is tied. Usually 30–45cm (12–18in) long.

Turn – One 360-degree path taken by a rope around an object or when coiled (p.17). To "take a turn" is to make a single round with the rope around an object such as a cleat, spar, bollard and suchlike.

Unlay – to separate the strands or yarns of a rope.

Whipping – the act of tightly wrapping small stuff around the end of a length of rope, to prevent it unlaying and fraying (p.17).

Working end – the part of the rope used in tying a knot (p.17).

Yarn – a number of fibres twisted together.

Z-laid rope – right-hand laid rope.

INDEX

Bold entries indicate
main knot references

PICTURE CREDITS

ACKNOWLEDGEMENTS

Firstly I must thank Des Pawson for introducing me to Quantum Publishing and providing me with the opportunity to write this book. I am also indebted to the many authors of my library of knot related books, which, to some degree, must have influenced my knowledge of the knots herein. Among them are Clifford Ashley, Geoffrey Budworth, Cyrus Lawrence Day, Bruce Grant, Hervey Garret Smith, Charles Warner and the unnamed authors of so many seamanship manuals published by various Government agencies around the world.

For that little extra knowledge that comes from sharing information by association, I am privileged as a member of the International Guild of Knot Tyers (IGKT) to have learned much from my peers through the pages of *Knotting Matters*, the Guild's quarterly newsletter. I have included the work of two fellow members in this book, Charlie Smith from Essex and John Smith from Surrey. My thanks to Marlow Ropes Ltd. for providing me with much of the cordage photographed in this book. Many of the artefacts and the backdrop for some of the photographs were kindly loaned by The "Starbolins", who, by re-enacting life at sea in a broadside mess in the late 1800s, teach knot tying at various shows and events, mainly to children.

Quantum Publishing would like to thank Peter Laws for jacket design, Celia Peterson and Gordon Perry for photography, Heather McCarry and Heike Löwenstein for illustration and Madeline Jennings and Jimmy Topham for editorial assistance.

ABOUT THE AUTHOR

Gordon Perry learned about knots in the late 1940s in his home town of Margate, first as a Cub, then as a Sea Scout and Sea Cadet. Practical experience came with shrimp trawling, lobster fishing and sea angling. A career spanning 40 years in the Royal Navy culminated in 1994 as a Lieutenant Commander. During this time, apart from the practical use of knots and rope, he practiced decorative ropework as a hobby.

Gordon is a long-standing member of the International Guild of Knot Tyers, and one-time editor of their magazine, *Knotting Matters*. He is now retired from the Royal Navy and works part-time as a Telecommunications Consultant. He was awarded the MBE in 1992.